Schliemann in Indianapolis

HEINRICH SCHLIEMANN

Courtesy of the Mansell Collection, London

Schliemann in Indianapolis

EDITED BY ELI LILLY

INDIANAPOLIS

INDIANA HISTORICAL SOCIETY

1961

Designed, printed, and bound
for the Indiana Historical Society
by The Lakeside Press,
R. R. Donnelley & Sons Company
Chicago, Illinois
and Crawfordsville, Indiana

A thin, small volume called *Tales of Troy*, translated from the German of Professor C. Witt by Charles De Garmo, and illustrated with a few of Flaxman's drawings of the *Iliad*, is responsible for the following study. That little book was read by the fourth or fifth grade class in old school No. 2, at Delaware and Walnut streets in Indianapolis. The interest of the children was intense, the girls became partisans of the Trojans while the boys warmly favored the Greeks. Many were the warm and not too logical arguments. Ever since then, the history, mythology, and art of the Greeks have been of top interest to this editor and led, among other things, to the following inquiry into the time that Heinrich Schliemann spent in Indianapolis, a hitherto almost neglected subject.

Without the substantial help of many persons, this record of Dr. Schliemann's sojourn in Indianapolis could not have been written. Of first importance was John N. Pantazides, of Athens, an importer and distributor, for it was he who arranged with the Schliemann heirs and with the Gennadius Library for access to the Schliemann manuscripts. He also secured the services of an able scholar, acceptable to both the family and the Library, to select from among the great volume of Schliemann papers those relating to the Indianapolis episode. Mr. Pantazides also helped in the careful planning of the work. His sudden death in May was a severe tragedy to us all. His son, Francis J. Pantazides, has been more than kind in continuing interest in this project.

Peter-Nick J. Vavalis, scholar and journalist, was the person chosen for the search among the Schliemann papers for those referring to Indianapolis, and a fine appointment it was. After examining some twenty thousand manuscripts, he furnished microfilms, photographs, typewritten copies in the original language, and where called for, English translations of the selected documents. It was he who first discovered that Schliemann's dissertation on the "Arabian Nights," included herein, had been sent to A. W. Hendricks.

We are deeply indebted to Dr. Peter Topping, at that time librarian of the Gennadius Library in Athens, for most valuable assistance and guidance, and to Mrs. Topping for giving us translations of the modern Greek letters in "American English."

To Miss Eurydice Demetracopoulou, assistant librarian, we owe sincere thanks, for not only did she co-operate in the quest most wholeheartedly, but it was she who discovered the diary which adds so much to our information.

Verlag Gebr. Mann, of West Berlin, publisher of Dr. Ernst Meyer's *Heinrich Schliemann Briefwechsel*, generously gave consent to our copying from Volume One of that work five of Dr. Schliemann's letters appearing there in English and to our translating two from the French and four from the German, a total of eleven in all. We are also indebted to the Mansell Collection, of 42 Linden Gardens, London, for generously allowing us to include the picture of Dr. Schliemann, which must have been taken about the time he was in Indianapolis.

Miss Margaret Way thoroughly searched the Indianapolis newspapers of the period. Mrs. Hazel Hopper and Miss Carol Deschler of the Indiana State Library, and Miss Caroline Dunn of the Indiana Historical Society Library were always helpful. C. Curtis Duck and Russell Furr located and furnished the records of the pieces of property owned in Indianapolis by Dr. Schliemann.

Howard H. Peckham, director of the Clements Library of the University of Michigan, made valuable suggestions. The work of Mrs. Vernice Cox and Mrs. Eva Rice Goble who prepared the manuscript is highly appreciated. Miss Gayle Thornbrough, able editor of the Indiana Historical Society, made many valuable additions and was the harbor pilot who steered the project to safe dockage. To all these good people, most humble and hearty thanks.

Last but far from least, I am thankful for the sympathetic attitude shown toward this work by Mrs. Andromache Melas, daughter of Heinrich and Sophia Schliemann, and by Leno and Alexander Melas, grandsons of the illustrious archaeologist. Mrs. Melas, at ninety years of age, and her sons are honored and respected citizen of Athens.

ELI LILLY

Contents

Illustrations

Youth and Mercantile Phase

Youth and Mercantile Phase

Heinrich Schliemann,[1] as is known by every one familiar with the lore, legends, and literature of ancient Greece, was the amateur archaeologist whose knowledge of Homer and whose imagination led to the discovery that the bare, denuded hill of Hissarlik in the Troad was the site of Troy. Up until then the preponderance of scientific opinion had favored the rise of ground near Bunarbashi, which was too far from both the Aegean Sea and the Hellespont to fit Homer's description in the *Iliad*. Previous to Schliemann's visit to the region, several other men had favored the Hissarlik location, among whom was Frank Calvert, an Englishman, serving as American vice-consul at the Dardenelles.[2] He owned a large portion of the hill but did not possess the resources to accomplish the tremendous task afterwards carried out by Dr. Schliemann. Calvert's generous and wholehearted encouragement and co-operation in the project was a very important factor in its success.

Heinrich Schliemann was born on the 6th of January, 1822, in a

[1] For biographical material on Schliemann the editor has relied mainly on the following items: Heinrich Schliemann, *Ilios, The City and Country of the Trojans* . . . (New York: Harper & Brothers, 1881); C. Schuchhardt, *Schliemann's Excavations* . . ., translated from the German by Eugénie Sellers (London: Macmillan and Company, 1891); Robert Payne, *The Gold of Troy* . . . (New York: Funk and Wagnalls Company, 1959); Emil Ludwig, *Schliemann: The Story of a Gold-Seeker* (Boston: Little, Brown and Company, 1931); John A. Scott, "Schliemann and Indianapolis," in *The Classical Journal,* XVII (1921–22), 404–6; *Encyclopedia Britannica,* XX (1959), 79.

[2] Frank Calvert and his brother Frederick had been residents of that locality for twenty years and owned large tracts of land in the vicinity of the supposed Troy, at Bunarbashi and Hissarlik. They both had done some archaeological work in the territory before the advent of Schliemann. Frank Calvert not only gave Schliemann permission to dig on his portion of Hissarlik, but also encouraged him in many ways, including advising him how to negotiate with the difficult Turkish government. He was an archaeologist in his own right, and had published dissertations on "The Asiatic Coast of the Hellespont," "Contributions Toward the Ancient Geography of the Troad," and "Trojan Antiquities."

little town in the German duchy of Mecklenburg-Schwerin. The first eight years of his life were spent among the sights and sounds of the village of Ankershagen in the same duchy. His father was the village pastor. The boy grew up with his mind filled with local traditions of mysterious and marvelous occurrences, vivid tales of the tragic burial of Herculaneum and Pompeii, and of the deeds of Trojan and Greek heroes. His youthful mind was equally as full of visions of that kind as was that of Don Quixote with dreams of knightly adventures.

At the tender age of seven or eight he fell violently in love with a darling little girl Minna Meincke, who shared his interests and they made many plans for the future, even, he says in his short autobiography, to excavate Troy.

His mother died when Heinrich was nine and the family of two brothers and four sisters was scattered among relatives with practically no means of support on account of serious trouble that his father had gotten himself into. Their former friends would have nothing to do with them and so Heinrich not only lost his mother but his "little bride" Minna, a blow that he felt to his dying day, or certainly until his marriage to Sophia Engastromenos.

Heinrich was sent to his uncle, the Reverend Friedrich Schliemann, pastor of the village of Kalkhorst in Mecklenburg. Here he had a teacher so competent that at Christmas, 1832, he sent his father a Latin essay upon the main events of the Trojan War. In 1836, when the boy was at the age of fourteen, the family income had shrunk so that Heinrich was forced to become an apprentice in a small musty-smelling grocery shop in the village of Fürstenberg in Mecklenburg-Strelitz. He worked there for five and a half years performing the usual menial tasks from five in the morning till eleven at night. In lifting a huge cask he injured his chest and suddenly began spitting blood. Since he could no longer endure such heavy work he went to Hamburg where his physical condition caused him to lose several positions.

Finally he shipped as cabin boy on the little brig *Dorothea* bound for La Guaira in Venezuela. He had to sell his coat to buy a blanket for the voyage. On the 28th of November, 1841, the ship sailed, only to be struck by howling gales and wrecked on the island of Texel in a wild December night of towering ice cold waves and flying black clouds.

Through the good offices of a friend in Hamburg, a subscription of twenty pounds was forwarded which helped him out of a desperate situation. With these funds he went to Amsterdam. There the Consul General of Prussia secured for him a position where he stamped bills of exchange, got them cashed in the city, and carried letters to and from the post office. His annual salary was thirty-two pounds. On half of this he lived in a dingy attic room while the rest was spent in improving his calligraphy and the study of the English and French languages. In a single year his unremitting toil had strengthened his memory to such a degree that the learning of Dutch, Spanish, Italian, and Portuguese proved very easy. It did not take him more than six weeks to write and speak each of these tongues fluently.

In spite of his extremely hard youth and his having had so little help from his family, he was loyal to them throughout life. No mention of his father's difficulties is made in his autobiography and he continually sent remittances to him and his sisters and brothers. To be sure, they were often accompanied by rather critical advice and biting admonitions, but he always responded to their appeals.

In March, 1844, he obtained a position as correspondent and book-keeper in the offices of Messrs. B. H. Schröder and Company and there he began building the foundation of his great prosperity. Seeing an opportunity to advance his commercial prospects in Russia, he applied himself in his whirlwind fashion to learning the language and in the usual six weeks was able to write and speak Russian. He then began to occupy himself seriously with the golden literature of the languages he had learned.

In January, 1846, his principals sent him as their agent through the glittering snow and cold to St. Petersburg and Moscow where his efforts "were crowned with the fullest success." Feeling himself finally well-established, he wrote a friend of the Meincke family begging him to ask for his childhood sweetheart Minna in marriage. The disastrous news that she had recently become a bride rent his heart to such an extent that he was prostrated with poignant grief and for some time was totally unfit for conducting business negotiations.

This crisis having passed, his business success in Russia was almost immediate and during the first year he was inscribed in the First Guild as a wholesale merchant. He retained his connection with the Schröder firm for eleven years. His chief interest in those early days was the buying and selling of indigo.

In the spring of 1850 Schliemann determined to join his brother Ludwig who had been drawn into the California gold rush. After terrific experiences crossing the steaming Isthmus of Panama, he arrived in Sacramento to find that his brother had died of typhus. With the 50,000 reichstalers he had taken with him, he established a gold-buying and banking business in San Francisco. He was there during the destructive fire of June 5, 1851. When he returned to Europe after an absence of eighteen months, he had more than doubled the capital that he had taken with him.

Although the fact is ignored in his autobiography which was published in the Introduction of *Ilios*,[3] in 1852 he was married to a Russian

[3]It was generally assumed that in this autobiography Schliemann deliberately omitted mention of his first marriage. However, according to Professor A. H. Sayce, who saw the book through the press, the publishers urged the omission of this phase of

woman, Catherine Lishin, who had repeatedly refused him while he was merely a successful merchant, but finally could not withstand the temptation of enormous wealth. Within a few disillusioning weeks he recognized that a terrible mistake had been made. Catherine proved to be a stubborn, ferociously frigid person who never gave him any affection and scant attention. She steadfastly refused to leave St. Petersburg under any circumstances. To Schliemann, whose life had to be spent in widely separated places, her position was a severe blow. He tried for years to change her attitude by entreaties, despairing letters, promises of palatial mansions and retinues of most proper servants and all that wealth could buy. Finally he resorted to threats of cutting her off and disinheriting their children Sergius, Natalya, and Nadezhda, all to no effect. This unfortunate situation, at long last, was responsible for Heinrich Schliemann's coming to Indianapolis in 1869.

But to return to him in Russia. He recounts that he was so busy establishing a branch house in St. Petersburg and in other business affairs that it was not possible for him to learn the Swedish and Polish languages until 1854.

In commercial matters he seems to have had the touch of Midas; his meticulous attention to detail, fury of initiative, and keen foresight unfailingly guided him throughout his business phase. He again doubled his capital during the Crimean War.

When the peace treaty was signed, he determined to carry out an ambition to learn Greek. One of his teachers was Theokletos Vimbos from Athens who afterwards became an archbishop there and later played an important role in Schliemann's life. Modern Greek was mastered in six months, and in three more the ancient language of Homer. The following two years he occupied his spare time in studying the Greek classics, especially the inspiring lines of the *Iliad* and "the surge and thunder" of the *Odyssey*. From then throughout life no matter what he was doing or reading, he could see, far beyond, the shining shield of Hector.

In the meanwhile his mercantile transactions in Russia went on steadily and favorably even through the depression of 1857. In the following year he reviewed Latin and found it easy going. Then he tried retirement from business, traveling through Sweden, Denmark, Germany, Italy, and Egypt. There he seized the opportunity to learn Arabic. He also visited Jerusalem, rock-bound Petra, the whole of Syria, Smyrna, the Cyclades, and glorious Athens in the summer of 1859.

He was unceremoniously brought back to St. Petersburg by a serious law suit. After its favorable settlement, he re-entered the commercial

Schliemann's life, not wanting it to be known that their new publication had been written by a divorced man, "divorce then being a relatively rare and unpopular occurrence in England." Roy C. Flickinger, "Sayce and Schliemann," in *The Classical Journal*, XXVII (1931–32), 24–25.

THE GENNADIUS LIBRARY,
American School of Classical Studies, Athens, in which
the Schliemann Papers are deposited

turmoil with his usual verve and intentness, dealing largely in indigo, olive oil, tea, and also cotton, made suddenly profitable by the American Civil War. His imports from May to October, 1860, reached £500,000.

The biographers of Schliemann usually portray him as a man whose sole ruling and all-consuming passion was the acquisition and accumulation of gold. This, it seems, is grossly unfair, for it was his nature to drive toward all his objectives in a frenzy of effort. Certainly his mastery of languages, his pursuit of archaeology, and most of his human relationships were of the same order. He simply lived the Homeric ideal, "to strive always for excellence and to surpass all others." An element of excess seems to be necessary to attain greatness.

Having found himself "in possession of a fortune such as [his] ambition had never ventured to aspire to," he liquidated his business and determined to see more of the world before devoting himself entirely to archaeology. So in April of 1864, he started for Tunis to investigate the ruins of Carthage, and from thence by way of Egypt to India, Ceylon, Java, China, Japan, and finally San Francisco. During the crossing of the Pacific he wrote his first book *La Chine et le Japon*. From the hills and bay of San Francisco he went by way of Nicaragua to the eastern United States, traveling through many of them. He also visited fragrant Havana and enjoyed the keen air of Mexico City. Then in 1866 he settled down in ever-attractive Paris to devote himself to the study of archaeology. He who studies this science is apt to contract a galloping disease.

In the winter of 1867-68 he was again in America, traveling by rail through the southern and Middle Western States, but in the early spring of 1868 he determined to begin active archaeological work, and started for Greece via Rome, Naples, and Corfu. He spent a day on Corfu where under resplendent skies of startling brightness he swam in the legendary stream by which Odysseus found himself after his last shipwreck and where he hid in the bushes and watched the beautiful Nausicaä and her maidens do up the palace laundry.

From there he continued his pilgrimage to seagirt Ithaca. With a field force of four men and a donkey he began his first "dig" at the supposed site of the palace of Odysseus. His party unearthed some vases filled with ashes and a sacrificial knife. With the enthusiasm always difficult for him to control, he wishfully thought that these ashes might be those of the old hero. Also by the same process, he found the stone walls of the sty of the faithful Eumaeus and possibly the very dunghill occupied by the old dog Argus.

From Ithaca he sailed for Corinth and made his way to Mycenæ, Argos, and Tiryns, all names that fill the mind with story and tradition. At Athens he found his old friend Archbishop Vimbos and in August he left for Troy by way of Constantinople. The story of how he poked disrespectfully at the shell rubbish heaps of denuded Bunarbashi and viewed 7 with clairvoyant perception Frank Calvert's small excavation at Hissarlik, is well known. He chose the latter as his long-sought Troy, but the season being late he wound up his expedition and began planning for next year's work.

His second book, *Ithaka, der Peloponnes und Troya,* was an account of this journey. The University of Rostock, to which he sent this dissertation, tendered him a doctor's degree of which he was always both proud and jealous.

But there was some very important unfinished business to be cleared away for his own peace of mind. Doubtless the romantic features in the stories of Homer had been running through his mind with extraordinary vividness during his Greek adventures, lightly turning his thoughts to those of love. At any rate, he began his plans for getting a divorce from his Russian wife and that is where the Indianapolis episode enters the picture.

After his usual careful and thorough consideration, Dr. Schliemann determined that if he were an American citizen, his necessary negotiations with the Turkish and Greek governments would be more successful than if he remained a German or became a Russian citizen. So he left Paris for America on March 13, 1869, arriving in New York on the 27th. There he completed his naturalization on March 29. While in New York, he learned that the divorce laws of Indiana were the most favorable to his intended course, and he set out for Indianapolis, arriving there on April 1, 1869. His diary and letters tell the story of his sojourn there.

Schliemann in Indianapolis

Schliemann in Indianapolis

Friday 26 March: Lat: 40.20′; Long. 72.58′; distance run 230 m; distance from N. Y. 155 miles. Only 6 degrees Celsius this morning in the bath.

New York 27th March: I took again a bath this morning temperature about the same. On account of the thick fog we proceeded on our voyage by 7 o'clock only, having stopt for the night. Got by 8 a pilot, passed Sandy Rock [Hook] by 9; splendid panorama of the Bay of New York with Long Island on the one and Staten island on the other hand, both, and particularly the latter, covered with magnificent villas; immense number of ships of all dimensions and also a great many tow and other steamers pass us whilst going up the bay. Landed only 2 P.M. on Canal-street-wharf. No difficulty at the Customhouse. Stopped at Astorhouse; carriage $1.50. Splendid accommodations at Astorhouse. Every where new costly carpets; excellent furniture; interior shutters instead of curtains. Wines dear; common Bordeaux $2 the bottle. Every hour new issues of newspapers with later and always later news from all parts of the world, cries of the newspaper boys. One look from the steamer on the houses adjoining the wharf; one ride or walk through a street satisfies a man that he is here in another world, for nothing is made here for outward show but all is only for practical purposes; in every house are wholesale stores, and of the bustle and business in the streets we are unable to make ourselves the slightest idea in the old world. In nearly every street are 2 and in many even 4 rails for the large City cars, which cross the town in all senses and directions and of which every one can take 50 passengers; fare 6 cents. Though french politeness is missing, there is nevertheless everywhere a . . . [illeg.] empressement to render service. The great nuisance here is that there are no pissoirs. Sundays very dull since all bars and places of amusement are shut. Servants all irish, since no american stoops to such an indignity as to serve.

11

N. York 29th March: I got today my paper as citizen of the U. S. Since no divorce can be obtained in the State of New York except on acct of adultery, whereas in Indiana even no previous residence is required[1] I have decided on going on 31st inst to Indianapolis. Peter Cook, the lawyer procures here divorce in a few weeks by false certificates and perjury; I will have nothing to do with such horrors. Messrs. [Mac] Killop Sprague and Co., 37 Park-row, Commercial agency, gave me letter to Geo E. Gordon,[2] lawyer of Indianapolis.

I examined with lawyer Moore 7 Chamber Street the laws of Ohio, Indiana, Illinois etc. in the law institute in Chamber street.

I went to see Doctor Th. Tellkampf 142 West 4th str, and G. Janssen; also L. von Hoffmann Co.

At the recommendation of Doctor Tellkampf I went to see the Reverend Howard Crosby and Doctor H. Drisler[3] 226 East 10th street; the latter being the greatest greek scholar here.

As a general thing classical litterature is despised here owing to the universal enthusiasms for acquiring material wealth; thus classical education is but on a very low ebb here; it cannot hold out the hard contest against the endeavors to acquire the knowledge to obtain material wealth. In the public schools greek and latin is not taught at all, but it is taught in the colleges of which there are 3 in N. Y. and in all 15 in the State of N. Y. Each has on an average 100 or 120 pupils divided in 4 classes. In the first classes the pupils read Plato, Sophocles etc. These colleges answer perfectly the german gymnasiums. There are here Universitary courses for medicine, law, theology & mining engineering, but there is none for philology.

[1] This was not actually true. The act regulating divorce as amended March 4, 1859, Section 1, stated: "Divorce may be decreed by the circuit courts of the State on petition filed by any person who, at the time of the filing of such petition, shall have been a *bona fide* resident of the State one year previous to the filing of the same, and a resident of the county at the time of the filing such petition, which *bona fide* residence shall be duly proven by such petitioner to the satisfaction of the court." *Laws of Indiana*, 1859, p. 108. There is no evidence that Schliemann established a residence in Indiana prior to April 1, 1869, but apparently he was able to circumvent the residence requirement. For further comment on this see John A. Scott, "Ludwig and Schliemann," in *The Classical Journal*, XXVII (1931–32), 20–21. Indiana at this time was known as an "easy place" in which to get a divorce, since by law divorce could be granted for any cause "which the court shall deem it proper." Efforts were being made to tighten the divorce procedure, as will be seen, and a new act was finally passed March 10, 1873. *Laws of Indiana*, 1873, pp. 107–12.

[2] This letter is in the Schliemann papers in the Gennadius Library. George E. Gordon is listed in the Indianapolis *Directory* for 1869 as a lawyer and also as a wholesale and retail dealer in dry goods, in the Odd Fellows Building. His residence was at 230 North Pennsylvania Street.

[3] The Reverend Howard Crosby (1826–1891) served as professor of Greek at Rutgers University and the University of the City of New York. Henry Drisler (1818–1897) was a professor of Greek and Latin at Columbia College and the author of widely used classical textbooks. *National Cyclopædia of American Biography*, IV (1897), 193, 254.

Doctor Drisler says the books published on Indian languages are:

Gallatin: researches on the American-indians 4 vol.

Buchanan: American indians 1 volume

Catlin: north american indians 2 volumes. All these books are likely to be got Nassau-street near Ann-street, at Gowen's[4]

W. W. Turner: on indian languages to be got gratuitously in the Smith[s]onian Contributions.[5]

A Convention of American Philologists will be held in Poughkeepsie, N. Y. commencing on Tuesday 27th July 1869.

I shall hurry off because *railway-accidents become epidemical here in spring.*

Tonight in the street Railway-car a boy, 8 years old stept in holding in his hand some dozens of small books with paintings, of which he laid a copy on the knees of every passenger singing out 2 cents a peace, 3 for 5 cents. It is wonderful indeed to witness how here such little boys are already caring for themselves and gaining their bread.

Indianapolis 8 April 1869. I left New York on Wednesday 31st ult by the Jersey Central RR. went afterwards on the Pennsylvanian RR. Had to pay $20 to Indianapolis and 3 $ for baggage and 2½$ for the use of a splendid sleeping car, called the Silver palace, as far as Pittsburg. There were in this car 11 silver columns; splendid silver lamps, in fact everywhere silverplated ornaments in great profusion; immense number of mirrors in silverplated frames, excellent toilettes, magnificent carpets, beautiful silken curtains; good waterclosets & stoves; excellent sleeping apparatus. I had good company and among the rest a lady of french descent and even born in France who had been married in New Orleans and, after her husband's death had married another man, of whom she severely complained, saying that he is a drunkard, constantly beats and otherwise illtreats her, so that she had fled from him on Holy Friday, when she had been severely ill-treated by her husband for not having prepared for him some meat, which he did not think sinful since he is from England, whereas she is of the catholic religion. I lamented her sad fate, but that was all I could do for her. She lives in Wisconsin and being without means she was returning to her husband.

Petroleum continues to be pumped on a large scale and in Pennsylvania alone at the tremendous rate of 8,000 barrels, at 40 gallons daily, which makes 116,800,000 gallons annually.

[4]Schliemann cites here: Albert Gallatin, *A Synopsis of the Indian Tribes within the United States* . . . (American Antiquarian Society, *Transactions and Collections,* II, 1-422, Worcester, Mass., 1836); James Buchanan, *Sketches of the History, Manners and Customs of the North American Indians* (1824); and George Catlin, *Letters and Notes on the Manners, Customs and Conditions of the North American Indians* . . . *1832–39* (2 volumes. 1842).

[5]Perhaps W. W. Turner's "Indian Philology," in Smithsonian Institution, *Sixth Annual Report,* 1851 (Washington, D. C., 1852), pp. 97–101.

We passed several rivers, among others the Tuskerawas, the Muskingo and the Ohio.

We crossed the Aleghany mountains, but I did not see an elevation higher than abt. 2500 feet

I arrived on Thursday 1 April at Indianapolis where I put up at the Bates-House, where the accommodation is certainly nothing like what it is in the Hotels of New York. Breakfast is from 6 till 10; dinner from 1½ till 2½; supper from 6 till 8. At both breakfast and supper the principal dish is buckwheat cakes with butter and molasses; besides eggs, ham, sirloin or porksteaks, etc. at all three meals tea or coffee is served. No wine is to be had and not even ale or porter. I therefore took some Whiskey at dinner but could take it but a few days, since it makes me too hot together with the heaps of pepper with which every dish is spiced. Both at table and in the rooms serve irish girls, who certainly do not appear to be types of virtue, but some of them are not bad looking. Indianapolis lies lat: 39.55'; long. 86.5' and 527 feet above the level of the sea; it is 827 miles from New York. But the temperature is here much lower than there and for several days we had severe frost. It is a growing city and crossed by 12 railways and their number will be 15 by the end of the year. After having resided for 5 days at the Hotel, I took the one story house No 22 on noble street[6] and got it furnished in a simple way, but still the furniture will cost abt. $200. I took a female cook who has half Indian and half negro-blood and her boy as servants. Close to my door pass 3 railroads, vis: [MS blank] and goods and passengers' trains are passing every moment, so that I hear almost continually the ringing of the locomotive bells. Nothing could give a better idea of this country's enormous traffic than those continual trains. But it ought to be borne in mind that Indianapolis is the central point of the roads going West. The streets are wide with broad trottoirs for foot passengers. The houses are well built and many are splendid.

I applied at once to the first lawyers' firm, that of Senator Hendricks, Hord and Hendricks,[7] at whose suggestion I took besides Seidensticker

[6] Schliemann rented this house from William H. English, who had purchased the property on October 1, 1866, from the Bellefontaine Railroad Company. It was located in the southeast corner of outlot 65, at what is now the northwest corner of East Washington Street and Noble Street (now College Avenue). The deed was not recorded until August 20, 1870. Information from C. Curtis Duck, president of The Spann Company, Inc., Indianapolis. William H. English (1822–1896) was an active figure in Democratic politics, a state legislator, Congressman for four terms (1853–1861), and candidate for the Vice-presidency in 1880. He was a banker and possessed large real estate holdings both in Indianapolis and outside Indiana. Jacob P. Dunn, *Greater Indianapolis* . . . (2 volumes. Chicago, 1910), II, 880–87.

[7] Later the firm of Baker, Hord, and Hendricks when ex-Governor Conrad Baker became a member, and finally the present firm of Baker and Daniels. Throughout the years it has been one of the top-flight law firms in the Hoosier capital. Hendricks, Hord,

and A. Naltner as attorneys at law[8] so that I have now in all 5 lawyers. I have just come in time to present my complaint to the 2d court on Monday last, 5th inst. for the court ajourns for nearly 2 months and only meets again on 1 June next. The principal tenor of my complaint is being published once a week, in a weekly paper, for the period of 51 days.[9]

Indianapolis 20 April. My female cook has left me with her boy the

---

and Hendricks of 1869 were Senator Thomas A. Hendricks, Oscar B. Hord, and Abram W. Hendricks.

Senator Hendricks was born near Zanesville, Ohio, in 1819, graduated from Hanover College, and began his law practice in 1843. He served as Democratic representative in Congress, 1851 to 1855, as Commissioner of the United States Land Office, 1855 to 1859, as United States senator, 1863 to 1869, and governor of Indiana, 1873 to 1877. He was Democratic candidate for the Vice-presidency in 1876, and was elected to that office with Grover Cleveland as President in 1884. He died in 1885. *Biographical Dictionary of the American Congress, 1774 to 1949* (Washington, D. C., 1950), p. 1298; *A Biographical History of Eminent and Self-Made Men of Indiana* . . . (2 volumes. Cleveland, 1881), I, D7:90–92.

Oscar B. Hord was born in Washington, Mason County, Kentucky, in 1829. He began to practice law in Greensburg, Indiana, in 1849, in partnership with James Gavin. Together they produced the Gavin and Hord *Revised Statutes of Indiana,* 1862. In 1864 he entered into partnership with Senator Hendricks in Indianapolis. He died in 1888. *Encyclopedia of Biography of Indiana* (2 volumes. Indianapolis, 1895, 1899), II, 127–29.

Abram W. Hendricks was born near Ligonier, Pennsylvania, in 1822. His father was an uncle of Thomas A. Hendricks. He was educated at Hanover College, Washington and Jefferson College at Washington, Pennsylvania, and Transylvania University. He practiced law in Rising Sun and Madison, Indiana. At the outbreak of the Civil War he organized the Jefferson County cavalry company, was elected captain, and came to Camp Noble in Indianapolis. He became paymaster of the states' volunteer forces, and served until mustered out in 1865 with the rank of lieutenant colonel.

In 1866 he joined the firm of Senator Hendricks and Oscar Hord. He died in 1887. Jacob Piatt Dunn, *Memorial and Genealogical Record of Representative Citizens of Indiana* (Indianapolis, 1912), pp. 268–72.

[8] The real estate and law firm of Adolph Seidensticker and Aegidius Naltner. The former was born in Göttingen, Hannover, Germany, in July, 1831. He landed in Baltimore in 1846, worked in Philadelphia on the *Freie Presse,* and came to Indianapolis in 1852. With others he founded the German *Telegraph* and the German Mutual Insurance Company of Indiana. From 1854 to 1860 he edited the Indianapolis *Volksblatt* and in the latter year entered the law and real estate firm of Kappes, Seidensticker, and Naltner. In the Civil War he was largely responsible for organizing the Thirty-second Indiana Volunteer Infantry, known as the German regiment. He was a member of the Indianapolis City Council from 1864 to 1869. He died in 1895. Dunn, *Greater Indianapolis,* II, 1223–25.

Naltner was born in Baden, Germany, and came to Indianapolis in 1851. He joined the firm of Kappes and Seidensticker, which became Seidensticker and Naltner. He later moved to Cincinnati where he died in 1891. Theodore Stein, *Historical Sketch of the German-English Independent School of Indianapolis "Our Old School"* (Indianapolis, 1913), p. 81.

[9] Apparently the notice appeared only in three weekly issues of the Indianapolis *Weekly Indiana State Journal,* April 9, 16, and 23, 1869. Section 11 of the Indiana divorce law provided that if "defendant is not a resident of the State, the clerk shall give notice of the pendency of such petition, by publication for three successive weeks in some weekly newspaper of general circulation. . . ." *Revised Statutes of Indiana,* 1852, pp. 233–38. 15

day before yesterday, of which I am really very glad, for she was of no account as servant, I could not rely upon her in any way, because she had too free habits, had a multitude of acquaintances, absented herself every moment, gave away my fine cigars to her lovers and wasted the money I gave her for the little household in the most wanton way. But all my endeavors to get another cook have hitherto been in vain and thus for more than two days I am quite alone in the house. My only consolation is that I keep a good glass wine, for I have excellent Rhinewine of 1865 and Assamanshäuser claret, the former at 18 the latter at 14$ a dozen. Until three days ago the weather was very cold and nasty, but last Sunday very warm weather has set in so that the trees are covering themselves with flowers and leafs.

Last night at abt. nine o'clock a hurricane accompanied by rain, hail and lightening came up and such was the fury of the wind that I was afraid the house would be knocked down. Scarcely had the storm lasted 5 minutes when a heavy shock was felt shaking the ground and plainly perceptible above the fury of the tempest. Soon after the fire alarm was sounded. I looked out but saw no fire. This morning I was terror-struck to see that the hurricane had knocked down the Central Railroad Freight Depot and burried 9 persons, who happened to be in the building at the time, but 7 of them were only slightly injured, whereas two—the night watchman Samuel Bell and Rev. Daniel Ballou, a Universalist minister, from Utica, New York who preached at Masonic Hall on Sunday night, were fatally injured and died soon after the accident.

The immense doors of the Depot were shut, but the wind blew upon those in front and entering the building with a terrible power blew it down. A vast number of other houses are more or less injured.

Today the weather is again much colder.

For some 10 days I have taken every morning a ride on horseback of 2 hours; but I see that in my monastic life it does me harm and I have therefore given it up.[10]

Mr. Egidius Nalkner, Mr. Seidensticker's partner, has yesterday gone to Cincinnati.

Indianapolis 3 May Mr. E. Nalkner has brought favorable news from Cincinnati.

I have not been riding for some weeks because I see it does me no good. On the 26th April I began to bathe in the river; the water is cold, but never mind; it appears to do me good.

On the 26th April was the anniversary of the foundation of the Oddfellows' society, in consequence of which great festival; great processions of the Oddfellows in their uniforms or grades of distinction in the streets, with many banners and music. Also the *Ladies* have a sort of Odd-fellows

[10]For an Indianapolis tradition associated with Dr. Schliemann's riding, see Appendix, p. 90, below.

NOTICE OF PETITION FOR DIVORCE,
In Indianapolis *Indiana Weekly State Journal*,
April 9, 1869

institution, whose members style themselves daughters of Rebecca; they also have distinctive ornamental dresses.

Very warm weather has at last set in.

A scoundrel having lately obtained a divorce in the Northern part of the State in the dirtiest and foulest way of his wife who had been living with him for upwards of 20 years, who had brought him some capital and who had enlarged it by her unrelenting labor, who had raised with him a number of Children and who had been nursing him with unremitting care during his late illness—the details of this abominable deed were made known by the public papers[11] and a full printed statement of them was presented to all the Senators and Representatives, who had lately been called together by the Governor of Indiana for an extraordinary session.[12] In consequence of this the public feeling was roused and a bill was presented on the 27th April in the Senate with an amendment to the existing divorce-law: that no divorce could be obtained unless the summons having bona-fide been presented to the defendant and unless a certificate was sworn to by two real estate holding citizens of the County in which the divorce was solicited that plaintif had been an actual resident of that county for three months when his complaint was filed;—besides heavy penalties to perjurers. This bill having passed the Senate with 23 yeas and no nays, it came to the House and was referred to a Judiciary-Committee, which returned it on 28th April with full approval. Since a clause is attached to this Bill that it has to come immediately into force it would necessarily delay my case if it passes the house, for it would take a long time to serve the summons to my poor wife. I therefore have been endeavoring to prevent its passage in the House in its present state.

I visited the Capitol both on 29th and 30th ult; in the Senate are abt. 45, in the lower-house more than 100 members.[13] In the latter the representatives behave much like school-boys, all chewing and continually spitting; many holding their legs continually on their desks before them and all putting the laws in the most summary and wreckless way.

[11] The Indianapolis *Journal,* April 6, 1869, carried the story under the heading "A Divorce Abomination," and observed that the "adaptability of the infamous divorce act to evasive construction, and its utter worthlessness for serving the ends of justice, is too potent not to claim the attention of the Legislature . . . ."

[12] The special session was called by Governor Conrad Baker to convene on April 8, 1869, since the preceding Regular Session had failed to provide necessary appropriations to carry on the state government and meet the current expenses of the benevolent and other public institutions. The reason for this was that on the day the Fifteenth Amendment to the U. S. Constitution was submitted to the Regular Session of the Assembly for ratification, seventeen Democratic senators and thirty-seven Democratic representatives bolted and any further legislation was impossible. This opposition again was to resign during the special session when the amendment was to be voted on, though only after the appropriation bill had been passed.

[13] Article 4, Section 2, of the Indiana Constitution of 1851, stated that the Senate should not exceed fifty members and the House not exceed one hundred members.

Certainly I should not like to live in a country whose welfare is entrusted to such fellows.

On the 26th ult. a girl of 10 or 11 y. coming from school wanting to cross the street just before the street car; was knocked down by the mule and ere the car could be stopped she was run over by the wheels of the car and killed on the spot.

Very cold and rainy weather set in on the 29th April and it lasted till late in the evening of 1 May. Even this morning (of 3 May) it was very cold, although the weather is exceedingly fine. The night before last I felt a terrible pain in my neck and could hardly breathe; must have taken cold.

Yesterday Sunday, 2d May, was a very tedious day, but I amused myself as well as I could in reading M. Brunet de Presle's "examen critique des dynasties egyptiennes."

My colored cook went to church yesterday morning at 9½, came home at 5½ P.M. left again for the evening service at 7 P.M. and only came back this morning at 7.

Indianapolis 17th May: The weather continues to be cold though every now and then there is a very warm day. The vegetation has rapidly advanced for the last two weeks and all trees are covered with splendid foliage.

What strikes me here is the enormous number of children, who, as a general thing, are very pretty and healthy. As one can here easily make a living nearly everyone is married and this accounts for the multitude of scions. But the great producers of children are the foreigners—germans and irish—, the americans being far less blessed with offsprings.

It is to be noticed that—as a general thing—the germans always marry ladies of their own nation and that the frenchmen always couple with irish women; probably on account of the religion.

Servants are very bad and always run out as soon as their work is done.

Since I was much afraid the Senate's divorce-bill Nos. 316 and 317 would pass in the Lower-House, I went there daily and remained there all the day. At last both bills were read on 11th inst. when representative Pierce requested to lay them on the table till the following morning, 9 o'clock, since he promised to present a substitute. On the 12th inst. his substitute was read;[14] it occupied ¾ of an hour, was thought to be too long and was laid on the table. Then the amendments were offered by the 24 democrats whom I had succeeded to get on my side through second

---

[14] The substitute bill which Representative Gilbert A. Pierce of Porter County presented provided among other things "that residence shall be held to mean only such persons as enter the State with the intention to take up their abode permanently; and when this is not proven, the cause shall be dismissed—if the party come into the State simply for the purpose of obtaining a divorce." *Brevier Legislative Reports,* special session, 1869, pp. 217–18.

hand; the first: to exclude pending suits was rejected; the 2d to strike out the word emergency could likewise not be sustained and by only one vote above ⅔ of the votes it passed that the constitutional rule should not be suspended and that the bill 316 was to be read a third time.[15] The following day, 13th May, to my greatest joy, 41 of the democratic members presented their resignations to the governor in order to avoid voting on the 15th amendment to the Constitution of the U. S. which gives to the colored people the right of voting.[16] By their resignation the House had no quorum and thus no more business could be transacted. The remaining abt. 60 republican members with but 3 democrats who had remained, voted then the 15th amendment, with but 3 nays (of the 3 democrats), but it is doubtful that the Congress of the U. S. can sanction this there not having been a quorum present in the House.[17] At all events no other business could be done by the House. My joy is immense. After all I am very glad to have got an insight into the doings of these people's legislative assemblies, which present Democracy in all its roughness and nudity, with all its party spirit and facility to yield to lateral influences, with all its licentiousness. I often saw them throwing paper-balls at each other and even at the speaker.

One meets here at every step men with only one arm or one leg and sometimes even such whose both legs are amputated. I saw even one whose both legs were amputated close to the abdomen. The disabled soldiers of this State come here to the Capital to receive their pensions and this accounts for the numberless lame men.

There are 93[18] Counties in Indiana.

The frenchmen married here to irish women are the slaves of the latter for the women are under the despotism of the clergy and take revenge on their husbands.

There are now 10 railways at Indianapolis and there will be 13 before the end of the year.

Among the boys selling newspapers there are some of only 6 years old who gain already their bread by useful industry.

I have been bathing here in the river for more than a month but it appears that there is no other amateur but me for early bathing.

There are no Coffeehouses here.

[15] These actions may be followed in *ibid.*, p. 218.

[16] The Amendment provides that the right of citizens of the United States to vote shall not be denied or abridged by the United States or by any State on account of race, color, or previous condition of servitude.

[17] On the vote on the Amendment the Senate may have had a quorum, but the House actually had only 56 members, and 67 were required to form a quorum. Fifty-four voted for ratification. The legality of the vote has never been adjudicated. John D. Barnhart and Donald F. Carmony, *Indiana. From Frontier to Industrial Commonwealth* (2 volumes. New York, 1954), II, 197–98.

[18] There were only 92 counties then as now.

19

Sunday is a very dull day here all shops being shut up except the segar depots.

Indianapolis 1 June 1869. Since the above was written we have had continually warm weather but not more than 80°. We have had tremendous rain storms and in consequence heavy inundation, which have nearly destroyed the bath at the bridge. The rainstorms are always accompanied by thunder and lightning and the newspapers are full of sad news abt. persons being struck dead or maimed by the flash of lightning.

Something marvellous are the innumerable suicides daily committed all over the country as reported by the papers.

The Pacific R.R. Co. charges 9 cents in gold per mile, which is treble what other roads charge.

The most disagreeable thing here is the Sabath-law, by which it is prohibited to grocers, barbers and even to bakers to open their shops on Sundays.

Here are fabrics where they manufacture horse-hair from bristles; but the principal fabrics are said to be at Baltimore.

The streets of Indianapolis are very wide and many of them 120 ft. broad; on both sides are broad sidewalks and altogether it is a fine city.

I am riding now again every morning.

My servant Harriet having come home lately after 1 in the morning I dismissed her on the 23d ult, but vainly endeavored since to find another colored woman to suit me. 4 at least I have had since then, but a good lady who lives next door to me, Mrs. Northerner, always persuades them to leave me right away. So I have now been compelled to take an old soldier, to whom I pay ½$ daily with victuals.

I intend leaving tomorrow morning for Fort Wayne whence I hope to return on the 5th inst.

Indianapolis 6 June: Since writing the above I got another lady servant, and though I allowed her to live at my house with her daughter aged 11 y: she was soon persuaded by my good neighbor to leave me and she only staid 1 day with me; she robbed me of a few dollars. I left on 2d inst. with Mr. Nalkner for Fort Wayne, but found the latter an exceedingly tedious place, for if there is very little to occupy the mind in Indianapolis there is literally nothing at Fort Wayne; but the city is well laid out and contains many good buildings and some fine churches and the streets are broad and have broad sidewalks of which some are paved with large flat stones. The streets proper are paved with wood in the following manner: the ground is first consolidated by stones and gravel; on this layer thick planks are laid which are abundantly pitched and on this pieces of oak abt. 1 ft. long, 4 inches broad and perhaps 8 inches high are ajusted, but so that there remains between them a space abt. an inch broad, which is filled up with gravel and pitch; this pavement is Nicholsen's patent. The climate in Fort

Wayne is certainly not healthy the place being surrounded by swamps, whose exhalations produce much fever, particularly in August and September. The city is situated at the junction of St. Mary's and Joe's river, both of which have produced just now great inundations. I could not discern their normal breadth on acct. of the overflow. Though the inhabitants boast that the population amounts to 35/m, I hardly think there can be more than 20/m. We stopt at the Aveline-House, which is very clean and in every respect well kept. Water is conducted into all the bedrooms and there is even running water at the bottom of the water-closets.

United States' Citizenship is granted in Indiana after one year's residence.

As an excellent and neverfailing remedy against Scarlet-Fever is much recommended and generally employed here to rub the whole body of the patient several times daily with bacon and to bind him . . . [illeg.] bacon round the neck. I heard of families where all the children died this remedy not having been resorted to, whereas I did not hear of one where a child died in spite of the use of bacon.

The jews cannot swear when their head is not covered and if they nevertheless do it they consider it no oath.

The principal street in Fort Wayne is called Calhoun-street; it derives its name from the great statesman of South Carolina, who already in 1836 attempted to separate the Slave-states from the Northern states.

The Americans are wonderful woodcutters; they cut 3 times more than anybody else; for one laborer (american) cuts daily 2 fathoms at 128 cubic feet each. They also excel in brick-laying and it is wonderful to see how a brick-mason lays in one day 2000 bricks into the walls of a building.

The iris[h]men are unsurpassed in public works in the streets and on Railroads.

The White River of Indianapolis falls into the Wabash river, which flows into the Mississippi.[19]

Indianapolis 30 June. To my greatest joy my divorce has been decreed today by the judge Samuel [Solomon] Blair; his only objection was that the children were unprovided for but as I consented to take them at my charge it was all right.

Two weeks ago I bought here for $1100 and $25 brokerage to A. Nalkner the house and lot No. 471 South Illinois street[20] and last week I

[19] The Wabash flows into the Ohio River which, in turn, flows into the Mississippi.

[20] The house stood on 33 feet and 3 inches of the south part of lot 31 in the Vanblaricum Subdivision of outlot 121 in the city of Indianapolis. It was bought from George and Margaret Ohleyer. The date of the deed was June 1, 1869, and it was recorded June 22, 1869. Schliemann did not keep this property, for it was sold by him and Sophia Schliemann to George W. Cox on September 5, 1873, the deed being recorded on September 12. Information from C. Curtis Duck, president of The Spann Company, Inc., Indianapolis. See below, pp. 63, 64.

bought here of Edw. Müller,[21] for $12,000-, his fourth share in the Starch factory on New York street, $350 Cash, the remainder to be paid on 25th July, with the express Condition that if I do not make the latter payment, the first is forfeited and the contract stands null and void.[22]

The weather has become very hot and the thermometer ranges between 22 and 25° Reaumur in the shade; the air is damp for it rains every day and thus it is very sultry and one feels the heat double.

I see here in the evening at every step bright sparks in the air, which are produced by the lightning bug; this latter is said to remain here only one month; the light is produced by the phosphoric matter, which the insect carries at its back part.

By the law of Indiana: "Statutes vol. II, article XXVIII, Section DLXXXVI, any person, who is a party to any judgement or the heirs, devisees, or personal representatives of a deceased party, may file in the Court where such judgement is rendered, a complaint for a review of the proceedings and judgement at any time within 3 years next after the rendition thereof. Any person under legal disabilities, may file such complaint at any time within 3 years after the disability is removed. But *no* complaint shall be filed for a review of a judgement of divorce."[23]

Indianapolis Sunday 11th July. Today the heat is very great; 25° Reaumur—88¼ Fahr in my room and much more in the street in the shade. I am preparing to leave on Thursday morning for New York.

New York Sunday 18th July: I got last Wednesday in Indianapolis a copy of the whole proceedings in my divorce case together with three copies of the decree.[24] The Court of Common Pleas broke up on the

[21] Edward Mueller is listed in the Indianapolis *Directory* for 1869 as a bookkeeper for the [Union] Starch Factory, with residence at 350 East Market Street.

[22] The Union Starch Factory, operated by the firm of W. F. Piel, Edward Mueller, Charles F. Wishmeyer, and Henry Burke, was located "at the east end of New York Street," close to Pogues Run and not far from the place where modern engineers have driven that stream ignominiously underground. The property was bounded by New York Street, Dickson Avenue, Marlowe Avenue, and Dorman Street. The plant, completed in March, 1868, burned to the ground on October 30 of the same year, at a loss of some $35,000. A three-story brick factory was built at once and, with a capacity of from 40- to 50,000 pounds of starch per week, resumed operation the middle of February, 1869. An article on the Union Starch Factory appeared in the June 26, 1869, issue of the Indianapolis *Daily Sentinel,* and the July 29, 1869, issue of the Indianapolis *Journal.*

The Diary entry, together with his letter to Émile Egger, July 11, 1869, below, pp. 49–51, shows conclusively that Dr. Schliemann never intended seriously to engage in the starch business.

[23] *Revised Statutes of Indiana,* 1862, II, 279–80.

[24] The divorce proceedings heard before the Marion County Court of Common Pleas were presumably conducted in the temporary courthouse constructed on the Court House Square in 1868. Dunn, *History of Greater Indianapolis,* I, 63. The official record of the proceedings is as follows:

"Marion County Court of Common Pleas, June Term 1869 . . .

following day and I left the same evening at 7½ by way of Columbus, Pittsburg, and Philadelphia and arrived at 7 o'clock yesterday morning in N. Y. It is here much cooler and only 82° in my bedroom.

The scenery on both sides of the R.R. was most delightful and particularly so in the Alleghany mountains.

The epidemy of railway accidents still continues and again a terrible disaster occurred on the Erie R. R.

The bustle and traffic in N. Y. really dazzles my mind and bewilders my understanding. The Commerce of the whole universe seems to be concentrated here. N. Y. consists of immense stone buildings 4 and 6 stories high, whose groundfloor is occupied by splendid stores and the upper stories by wholesale dealers. At every step the streets are crossed by immense numbers of telegraphic wires and uninterrupted lines of street cars capable of holding 24 persons run along the immense thoroughfares. I visited to day several large quarters of the city which but a few years ago were covered by the tide. N. Y. is already now more than 6 miles long and has at least 1,200,000 inhabitants and its population is bound to increase to 5,000,000 in 50 years hence.

Since the rooms are much higher than those of Paris the houses are also much higher than those of the Capital of France.

I have got my ticket transferred to the steamer St. Laurent of the 24th inst.

Henry Schliemann vs Catherine S.
Divorce *April 3, 1869*
Dedimus issued
June 26 Proof of pub. filed. Defendant defaulted.
June 30 Sub. to court for trial. Decree of divorce to Plff.
and he is hereby charged with the comfortable support and maintenance of all his minor children.''

LETTERS OF DR. SCHLIEMANN

[*Original in German*]¹
TO COUSIN ADOLPH SCHLIEMANN, SCHWERIN

Indianapolis,
April 11, 1869

. . . Although here only for a brief time, I have settled quite domestically, as I cannot bear hotel life; I have a black servant and a black cook, half of Indian and half of Negro blood. . . .

How happy would I have been here in this bustle of commerce, among these practical Americans, had I come here 27 or even only 24 years ago! But coming here after having for a lifetime pursued a difficult career in Europe and amassed wealth at it, and particularly after having tasted the wonderful life of Paris for 2½ years and, in continuous striving for beauty, arrived at living only in metaphysics, then naturally it is not possible to feel at home here, and, of course, one longs to be back in Europe. . . .

[*Original in German*]²
TO FATHER, SISTER AND BROTHER-IN-LAW IN LYCK

Indianapolis in the state of Indiana,
April 11, 1869

. . . The cook reads 3 large newspapers daily and is completely versed in the politics, history and geography of the country and may this give you an idea of the education of the people here, when you consider that in the entire state of Indiana there is not yet a single school for colored people (descendants of Negroes) . . . . but popular education is wholly, entirely practical and there is no trace of obedience. But because everyone from childhood on is instructed to think for himself, progress is achieved and results are obtained here in commerce and industry of which

¹Translated by permission from Dr. Ernst Meyer, *Heinrich Schliemann Briefwechsel* (Berlin, 1953), I, 145.
²Translated by permission from Dr. Meyer, volume I, 145–46.

not the faintest concept can be had by conditions in Europe. So, for example, 12 great railroads come through this little town of 40,000 inhabitants and their number will increase to 15 before the end of the year. Three railroads go right by my house and the clanging of trains arriving and departing continuously from early morning till late at night gives evidence of the really colossal traffic on these.

As everywhere in America, so here, too, the Germans are greatly respected for their industry and assiduity as well as their solidity, and I cannot think back without alarm of Russia where the foreigner, and the German in particular, is despised because he is not a Russian . . . .

[*Original in Greek*]   Indianapolis of the state of Indiana
of the United States of North America,
13 April 1869

TO THE MOST HOLY ARCHBISHOP OF MANTINEIA AND KYNOURIA,
THEOKLETOS, ATHENS.

Dearest Theokletos![3]

Regarding my letter to you from Paris on March 12, I hasten to inform you that after a pleasant 14 day voyage I arrived at New York on March 27. Having obtained there my official documents as a citizen of the United States,[4] I continued my journey to Indianapolis, because I had learned that divorces are more easily obtained there than in any other place. The lawyers here form firms of three members belonging to the various political parties. They do this to insure themselves clients from all political factions. You will surely believe, without my taking an oath, that I directed myself to the 3 leading lawyers of the capital.[5] One of these was for many years a senator in Washington. . . . He therefore enjoys a very high reputation. Because my case is somewhat complicated I retained, on the advice of the lawyers already engaged, two more lawyers. Thus, strange to say, I have now 5 lawyers. By the grace of God I arrived here towards the end of the court session, so that I was able to present my petition before the beginning of the recess, which lasts until June 1. My suit is now being published for 51 days in a weekly journal,[6] and will certainly be judged early in June. None of my 5 lawyers doubts that the judge will grant me a divorce without any hesitation. If I had arrived just 2 days later, I could not have presented my petition before the beginning of August, and then it would have been judged only in October.

. . .

I remain always with respect and love your former pupil,

HENRY SCHLIEMANN

[3] See reference to Archbishop Vimbos, above, p. 6.
[4] See below, p. 53.
[5] See Diary entry, above, pp. 14–15.
[6] See above, p. 15.

[Original in Greek]

Indianapolis, Capital of
the State of Indiana.
14 April, 1869

TO MR. EGGER,[7] MEMBER OF THE FRENCH ACADEMY IN PARIS.

Honorable Scholar:

. . . I discovered in New York only two scholars, the clergyman Howard Crosby and Doctor H. Drisler,[8] who is known in the New World as a very great Hellenist. He is well acquainted with all your writings, and with almost all that has been written by the Hellenists of France and Germany. He told me that classical philology is generally scorned in the United States of America because of the universal passion for gaining material wealth. Therefore, classical education is at a low ebb. It cannot compete against efforts to learn practical skills for the acquisition of wealth. In public schools the students do *not* learn any classical language whatsoever. But Greek and Latin are taught in the high schools. There are 3 such schools in New York. Each high school has 100 pupils divided into 4 classes. The pupils of the first class read Plato, Sophocles etc. Dr. Drisler says that these schools correspond exactly to the *gymnasia* of Germany. University courses exist only for medicine, theology, law and metallurgy, but *not* for philology.

. . . Here in Indiana classical education does not exist at all. I saw in a bookstore an American edition of the first 7 books of the *Iliad* and another book containing part of *Cyrus' Anabasis*. There was no other Greek book. On the contrary, I found in the above-mentioned bookstore Virgil, Horace, Tacitus, and Julius Caesar. I am assured that children here begin Latin with reading Virgil. So General Mansfield,[9] the best educated man here, told me. As he is a serious person, he speaks the truth.

---

[7] Émile Egger (1813–1885), philologist and classicist, and professor of Greek at the University of Paris.

[8] See above, p. 12n.

[9] John Lutz (later Mansfield) was born in Braunschweig, Germany, in January, 1803, and came to the United States in 1824. He spent some time in Madison, Indiana, then the metropolis of the state, and became professor of mathematics at Transylvania University, in Lexington, Kentucky. There he married a Miss Mansfield and took her surname. He returned to Indiana, near Madison, in 1850. During the Civil War he was a brigadier general of the Indiana Legion and served for a short time as colonel of the 54th Indiana Regiment. He moved to Indianapolis in 1866. In 1871 he founded Mansfield, Illinois, twelve miles northwest of Urbana (population in 1950, 665), and died there in September, 1876. He was of the big hearty German type with kindly eyes and a full beard—very full indeed. Gustave P. Koerner, *Memoirs . . . 1809–1896 . . .* (2 volumes. 1909), II, 348, 355, 364–65; biographical notes in Indiana Historical Society Library.

Just now they are recommending to me as a good Hellenist a certain clergyman, S. K. Hoschour[10] by name. I shall visit him at once, and at the end of this letter I shall tell you the result of our conversation.

Because I dislike living in a hotel, I have rented a small house here for 3 months.[11] I have furnished it, and hired a colored servant and a cook whose mother was an Indian and her father a negro. Three railroads are located 100 metres from my house, and the endlessly coming or going steam engines bear happy testimony to the magnitude of commerce. Just imagine—Indianapolis, a city of only 40,000 inhabitants, has 12 railroads. This number will increase to 15 before the year's end. But believe me, though I am not swearing an oath, there is nothing here for the intellect, and unfortunately I am much too distraught for serious philological studies. Just as I write these lines I receive from Dr. H. Drisler in New York the programme of a convention of American philologists . . . .

[Original in French][12]

TO ERNEST RENAN, PARIS[13] .

Indianapolis, Indiana,
April 14, 1869

Sir, I promised to write you as soon as I found anything very unusual to tell you.

In this country, I had often seen gigantic enterprises and paradoxes, independent men of 13 and 14 years of age; but the other day I saw, in

[10]Samuel K. Hoshour was a pioneer educator and linguist of more than local reputation. He had been born in York County, Pennsylvania, in December, 1803, trained as a Lutheran minister, was converted to the "Campbellite" doctrine, and migrated to Centerville, Indiana, in 1835. He taught in the Wayne County Seminary for four years. At the end of his first year there, he was made a trustee of Indiana University. Three of his pupils at Centerville were George W. Julian, Oliver P. Morton, and General Lew Wallace. His next charge was a similar school at Cambridge City, Indiana. In 1858 he became the first president of North-Western Christian University, now Butler University, which was then located in the block on the east side of College Avenue and north of Thirteenth Street. He served in this capacity for three years, and then for fourteen years was professor of foreign languages and Bible literature, teaching French, German, Latin, and Greek. He was popular and highly respected and admired by his pupils and the public.

In 1862 he served for a few months as state superintendent of public instruction, during which time he called a state convention of school examiners which outlined features that were later adopted into the school system. Dr. Hoshour died late in November, 1883, and was buried in Crown Hill Cemetery. Madison Evans, *Biographical Sketches of the Pioneer Preachers of Indiana* (Philadelphia, 1864), pp. 220–46; James H. Smart, *The Indiana Schools and the Men Who Have Worked in Them* (Cincinnati, n.d.), pp. 92–93.

[11]See above, p. 14.

[12]Translated by permission from Dr. Meyer, I, 146.

[13]Ernest Renan (1823–1892), a French philosopher and orientalist, was born at Trequier and graduated at the college there, winning all the prizes in 1838. He studied   27

New York, an 8-year-old businessman who supported himself as well as a large family through his industry. I was in a streetcar (horse-drawn wagon on rails) when a small boy came in holding a stack of brightly illustrated booklets under his arm. He placed one of them on the lap of each of the 24 passengers and shouted: "Only two cents a piece," while at the same time he whispered in their ear: "But *you* shall have 3 for 5 cents." After having thus distributed 24 copies of the booklet he again made the rounds either to collect his money or to take back his book. My boy, I said, you are quite a young businessman, how old are you? I have just completed my eighth year, he replied, my father died last year and left a sick wife and 6 children, of whom I am the eldest, and so I was compelled to do business to support the family. Here is a dollar, I said, do take it as a present. Sir, said the boy seriously, I am a merchant but not a beggar; I will not take your money unless you accept 60 books from me. Amazed and astounded to find such self-respect in an 8-year-old child I took the 60 books which he was counting for me with scrupulous accuracy and in taking leave I said to him: May this dollar be the foundation stone to your earthly fortune, my boy; may you one day become a great banker, the pride and glory of this great country, which, with such characters as yours, is bound to eclipse all the empires emblazoned in history. . . .

[*Original in English*][14]

TO FRANK CALVERT,[15] DARDANELLES

Indianapolis in Indiana,
14. April 1869

. . . With the excavations at Hissarlik I think we must wait till next spring for I cannot hope to obtain my divorce here before the beginning of June and thus I cannot be back at Paris before end of June and the terrible heat, and the pestilential fevers and the dryness of the soil make the works next to impossible in the summer months.

for the priesthood in the convent of St. Nicholas in Chardonnet but broke with that life and became an usher in a boys' school. He was sent to Italy by the government on a scientific quest and then given a small post in the National Library. His doctorate was achieved in 1852. At the time he thought nothing less important than prosperity. He was married in 1856, translated the Book of Job and the Song of Songs in 1859, and became a notorious heretic. In 1860 he went on a Phoenician archaeological expedition. In 1862 Renan was elected to the chair of Hebrew at the Collège de France, but was suspended after his first lecture because he said Christ was "an incomparable Man." A librarian's post was then refused by him, and thereafter he lived by his pen. His *Life of Jesus,* for which he is most widely known in this country, is said to be hardly a work of great scholarship. He wrote the *Apostles* in 1866, and *St. Paul* in 1869. He then experienced a period of disenchantment and bitterness followed by a mellowing as is usual with the accumulation of years. *Encyclopædia Britannica,* XIX (1955), 144–45.

[14] From Dr. Meyer, I, 147, by permission.

[15] See above, p. 3.

All the questions you make me as to the tumuli of Penti caparum and the publications on the "Lares et Penates" found 20 or 25 years ago in the excavations at Tarsous, I have immediately sent to my friend Mr. Ernest Renan of Paris, whose answer I shall promptly send you. . . .

[*Original in English*]

TO E. W. SCHLIEMANN, BORDEAUX

Indianapolis in Indiana,
14 April 1869

My dear brother:

I am in receipt of your kind letters of 12th and 25th ult. and I thank you for your wishes for a prosperous journey, which have so far been fulfilled because I have never yet made a more agreeable passage across the ocean than this time though we had continuous storms. My only displeasure was that I must not get seasick and yet my appetite was always too voracious.

Our views respecting matrimony do most decidedly not agree, for I consider that marriage is one of the noblest and most holy institutions if its only bonds are love and virtue but that it is the most degrading and the heaviest of fetters if taken by interested motives. You think differently of the matter; let me therefore drop it and not speak any more about it.

. . .

No sooner had I left the shores of France than the thought struck me that in this great country and among this practical people a divorce can impossibly require more than a couple of months, and in fact I found it so here, because marriage is considered here merely as a civil contract which must cease to exist so soon as it is violated by one of the contracting parties. Thanks to Heaven I arrived here just in time to present my complaint before the recess of the Court which lasts until end of May; had I come two days later I could have presented my complaint only in June and it would not have been decided before August or September whereas now I confidently hope that it will be decided in June so that I can return by the French steamer of 12th June. I have taken the five most distinguished lawyers of this city and certainly I have no doubt of my prompt success.

I am exceedingly sorry to have taken out here for so short a time 1000 of my fine Havana segars, on which I have had to pay $ [illeg.] duty; and I am still much more sorry to have given you order for two Casks of wine, because though you invoiced them to me more than a month since I have not heard yet of their arrival at N. Y.; and besides I do not know what I shall do with this enormous quantity of claret on which the duty and charges will not fall short of $ [illeg.], and I shall never be able to sell it here the article being hardly known here by name. 29

But certainly in so doing it I had no idea that my case could be decided so soon. Sound reason came when I had left the french shore and then it came too late.

I need not telling [sic] you that there is no resource here for the mind; but nevertheless I do not feel tedious.

Indianapolis has only about 40,000 inhabitants, but nevertheless it is crossed by 11 and before the end of the year by 25 railroads.

If contrary to all expectations I lose my suit here I institute forthwith in June a new one for divorce in Wisconsin then I shall have to stay in Milwaukee perhaps until the end of the year. But I do not expect it will come to that. If I succeed here then I hope to spend the summer in Switzerland or in the Pyrenees; in this lucky case your letters from Bordeau until 13th May will find me still in America but not later.

Good bye. Your faithful brother

H SCHLIEMANN

[*Original in Greek*]

Indianapolis,
26 April 1869[16]

TO THE MOST REVEREND ARCHBISHOP OF MANTINEIA AND KYNOURIA, THEOKLETOS, ATHENS.

Dearest Theokletos—

Confirming my last letter to you written on the 13th, I now take pleasure in notifying you that I have received your letter from Athens written 15/27. With sorrow I see that you find yourself before a chasm of the money lenders, which chasm threatens to devour you. You must be paying them a monthly interest of 2 per cent, perhaps even more. Thus your concern over money matters oppresses you and impedes you in the performance of your professional duties. I swear to you I never lend money to *anybody* because, as the proverb puts it, if you want to turn your friends into enemies, just lend them money.

But I love you as if you were my own true son. I hold you in great honor, and I am convinced that you would rather die than break a promise. For this reason I am unwilling to leave you in your present oppressed and harassed state, and I hasten to write to my banker in Paris, the General-Consul of Greece, M. Emile Erlanger & Co., to send you, on my account, Fr. 10,000, the sum you require. You promise to repay this sum by installments in 2 years. To facilitate your payments, I beg you to make the remittances to my account in the Hellenic Bank. Instead of monthly interest at 2 or 3 per cent, as you now pay the money lenders, you will pay 4 per cent *annually* to your noble and admirable sister, to whom I

[16] Apparently Schliemann did not send this letter, though it is in his copybook. He must have reconsidered, and mailed instead the letter immediately following.

30

SOPHIA SCHLIEMANN

make a gift of the interest. Write me the name of your sister—it is still unknown to me—and tell me the sex and name of the child which God has given her.

I think that I shall obtain my divorce on May 26.

I still have no information from the university as to whether they will give me the desired title of doctor.[17] Since I have received the pictures[18] you sent me, under no circumstances will I marry the cousin about whom I wrote to you. If she should accept my proposal, then I shall immediately send her a good dowry to enable her quickly to find another fiancé.

As I am an old traveler and a good reader of faces, I can tell you right away the character of the 2 girls from their pictures. Polyxena Gousti's surname shows that her ancestors were Italian. *Gousti* is an Italian name, *not* Greek. Her age is that which is suitable for my wife, but she is bossy, imperious, domineering, irritable and resentful. I imagine that she has acquired all these faults in her unenviable profession as a teacher. But I could be mistaken; perhaps if I saw her face to face, I might discover in her a treasure of all the virtues. As for Sophia Engastromenos, she is a splendid woman, affable, compassionate, generous, a good housekeeper, lively and well brought up. But, alas, she is too young for a man of 47 years. It seems to me that I saw her in Athens. Is she perhaps the daughter of your relative the broker?

I think it would be better for me to marry a young widow of exemplary behavior, who already knows what marriage means. Furthermore, she would be less voluptuous and sensual, while young girls believe that heaven and paradise lie in the fulfillment of their physical desires. And I, my friend, used to be very sensual and sentimental. But my character has completely changed. I live now only in a metaphysical world, and I think of nothing except scholarship. Therefore I want a wife only for companionship. I add that my wife must have a great inclination towards learning, otherwise she will not be able to love and honor me. Try to find me a wife with a Greek name and a soul impassioned for learning.

[17] In his Autobiography Schliemann wrote, "Having sent a copy of this work ["Ithaka"] together with a dissertation in ancient Greek, to the University of Rostock, that learned body honoured me with the diploma of Doctor of Philosophy. With unremitting zeal I have ever since endeavoured to show myself worthy of the dignity conferred on me." Schliemann, *Ilios*, p. 20.

[18] In February Schliemann had written to his friend the Archbishop, asking him to find for him a Greek girl who would be his wife. " . . . if you can send me the portrait of the girl whom you destine for me, so much the better. I entreat you: choose for me a wife of the same angelic character as your married sister. She should be poor, but well educated, she must be enthusiastic about Homer and about the rebirth of my beloved Greece. It does not matter whether she knows foreign languages or not. But she should be of the Greek type, with black hair, and if possible, beautiful. But my main requirement is a good and loving heart." Quoted in Emil Ludwig, *Schliemann*, pp. 111–12.

Also, I beg you to write me who was Polyxena's father; what was his profession; when did her mother and father die; how many years has she taught; and what subjects she teaches, and how old she is; to what studies does she incline; does she know our ancient language?

Please write to me in Paris, because I think your reply will not find me still in America.

> HENRY SCHLIEMANN
> 6, Place St. Michel, 6
> Paris

In anticipation of your good news, I embrace you respectfully and lovingly, your former pupil

> HENRY SCHLIEMANN

[*Original in Greek*]

> Indianapolis,
> 26 April 1869

TO THE MOST REVEREND ARCHBISHOP OF MANTINEIA AND KYNOURIA, THEOKLETOS IN ATHENS.

Dearest Theokletos—

Confirming my last letter to you written on the 13th, I am now delighted to announce the receipt of your most honorable letter of the 15/27.

Dearest friend of my heart, 23 years ago I loaned 400 francs to a man. But he never repaid me a single penny. At that time my whole estate consisted of those 400 francs. Therefore my excessive grief led me to swear a mighty oath in church that I would never again lend money to anyone. When the other day I wrote from Paris urging you to open your heart to me and to tell me the sum of money which you urgently needed so that I might lend it to you, I then expected you to speak of 1000 francs, and I intended to give them to you as a gift, and not as a loan. But the sum you require is large, and since—to my sorrow—I cannot lend money without becoming a perjurer, I am limited to sending you the enclosed 1000 francs. I beg you to accept them as a *gift* from me.[19]

Please be so kind as to write me the name of your honored sister, which I still do not know. Also tell me how she is, and the sex and name of the child which God has given her.

I think that I shall obtain my divorce on $\frac{\text{May 26.}}{\text{June 7}}$

I have as yet no information from the German university as to

___

[19] On the same date Schliemann instructed his bank in Paris, E. Erlanger & Co., to pay to Archbishop Vimbos, 1,000 francs and charge the payment to Schliemann's account. Vertical note on pp. 45–46 of the copy press letter book for 1869.

32

whether they will grant me the title of doctor, which I want. After the receipt of the pictures which you sent me, I do not want under any circumstances to marry that cousin about whom I wrote to you. If she accepts my proposal, then I shall send her a good dowry to enable her to arrange at once another marriage. As I am an old traveler and a good reader of faces, I can tell you right away the character of the two girls. . . .

[Original in Greek]

Indianapolis,
27 April 1869

TO ARCHBISHOP THEOKLETOS VIMBOS, ATHENS

Most Reverend Friend,

    With my letter of yesterday I sent you 1000 francs drawn on my Paris account. I begged you to accept this remittance as a token of my love for you. My friend, already (I have fallen in love with) Sophia Engastromenos . . . so that I swear she is the only woman who shall be my wife. But please do not say anything about this to anybody, not even your sister. For two reasons I don't know yet whether I am in a position to marry: first, I am not yet sure that I shall get the divorce; second, because of my matrimonial (difficulties) I have had no relations with a woman for 6 years. . . . And if then I am convinced that I am fit, then I shall not hesitate to go to Athens and talk with Sophia, whom I shall marry if she consents. We are forced to wait until then, because if I am impotent . . . I should not marry. Yes, as much as a woman may love her husband before marriage, she will always despise him if he is unable to gratify her physical passion.

    Naturally I do not want a wife with a dowry. On the contrary, if I am physically fit, and propose marriage to Sophia in July, then I shall buy her underclothes and stockings. Nevertheless I beg you to answer the following questions.

1. *Who is* Engastromenos? What is his *property?* How *old* is he and *how many children has he?*
2. *How many male and how many female? What is the age of each?*
3. *Particularly, how old is Sophia?*
4. *What color is Sophia's hair?*
5. *Where does this family live in Athens?*
6. *Does Sophia play the piano?*
7. *Does she speak any foreign languages? Which?*
8. *Is she a good housekeeper?*
9. *Does she understand Homer and our other ancient authors? Or is she totally ignorant of our ancestors' language?*
10. Would she agree to change her residence to Paris, and to accompany her husband on his journeys to Italy, Egypt and elsewhere?   **33**

I warmly beseech you to give me *precise answers* to all these questions. Send your letter to Paris.

I hope to arrive in Paris around June 25. For this reason be sure to write me early in June.

Are you satisfied with your new high vocation?

In anticipation of your good news, I offer you my respects with love.

Your former pupil
HENRY SCHLIEMANN

[Original in German][20]

TO ADOLPH SCHLIEMANN, SCHWERIN

Indianapolis, May 8 [1], 1869

. . . I will help you this time; but you must swear to me that never again in your life will you take cards into your hands. . . . They know that any contact with cards kindles anew the old passion in you; they know that by this passion you bring destruction to yourself and ruination to your poor dear family—how then should they not renounce with true joyfulness of heart playing cards with you. Yes, it is their holy duty to do everything in the world to keep you from it. How can a scholar like you only play cards anyway? Is there anything sillier, anything more materialistic than playing cards? Is there anywhere in the world a peasant incapable of playing cards? Truly, nature has not endowed you with these exceptional intellectual gifts that you may trample on them and bring about your and your family's ruination by surrendering yourself to the basest depravity of the lowest classes. Instead of playing cards, why don't you sit down with the people and tell them something; take an hour for preparation of such stories. You yourself, as learned as you are, can only grow through such prepared stories (and entertain) all your listeners a hundred times more than you would ever be able to do with the most ingenious card games. Thus, only on condition that from now on no cards shall be touched will I help this one more time. . . .

[Original in Greek]

Indianapolis, 15 May 1869

TO MR. ISIDOROS SKILISSIS, PARIS

Most Honorable Friend

I beg your pardon for not writing to you much sooner. I kept postponing this pleasure from one week to the next so that I could tell you definitely when I would obtain the divorce. Luckily I arrived here near the end of the court session; but there was still time for me to present my suit. Thus it will be heard early next month. Since I have retained

34   [20] Translated by permission from Dr. Meyer, I, 147–48.

the five leading lawyers, and have, I think, all the evidence required here, I did not doubt that I should soon be free. But suddenly, out of the clear, dark clouds covered the heavens, and for four or five weeks I lived in great fear of not attaining my goal before September. This is what happened.[21] Some years ago a scoundrel married a lovely, rich girl whose tireless efforts substantially enlarged her husband's estate. The couple had many children (seven I believe), and gave the appearance of living in complete harmony. After 21 years of married life, the man fell in love with another young woman. He goes to another county of Indiana (I should explain that this state has 93 [92] counties, each of which has courts entitled to grant divorces), and through false witnesses and perjured proofs he wins a divorce. Meanwhile his unhappy wife hasn't the slightest knowledge of the affair. After a divorce has been granted, nine days must always elapse during which the divorce may be contested and invalidated. However, after this deadline, the divorce is valid even though the wife presents the court with most positive proofs that he won the divorce by perjuries and false witnesses. In spite of all this, the wife is then forced to leave her husband's house immediately, and all her property along with the children belong to the husband. As I mentioned above, this scandal occurred early in April in one of Indiana's northern counties. As the wife was very highly respected, the news at once spread throughout the country, and was reported in all the newspapers. But no one, except the legislature, can change the law. This body convenes once every two years. And since the last session took place last January, the next session was due only in January 1871. An accumulation of many matters caused the governor to call a special session of the Senate and House at the beginning of April. And one of the first proposals in the Senate was a new divorce law, which would in many ways obstruct my case. The senators' indignation brought immediate passage of this bill. But before it could become law, the House must also pass it. It was my good fortune that the House had before it thousands of matters so that the new divorce bill was presented in its turn only yesterday. I had worked for many weeks to arouse opposition against the bill in the House, or at least to delete the two words "most urgent," without which the law would go into effect only in September. Failing this, I hoped to have pending cases exempt from the law. But since I could not personally speak to the legislators, and had to act always through others, I succeeded in winning only . . . to my side. Thus, day before yesterday, all my corrections were rejected, and I *barely, barely* succeeded by a one vote majority in maintaining the constitutional order and in postponing the bill for a new reading. Yesterday the new bill would certainly have been read again and become law had not the Almighty showed me great favor. The sessions adjourned

---

[21] For a discussion of this matter see above, p. 17.

yesterday morning because of party rivalry. Therefore the old divorce law is completely valid at least until January 1871. So I have hopes of getting my divorce about June 10, and of arriving in Paris early in July . . . .

. . . I am most anxiously waiting for the moment when I can leave this place. My position here is indeed very unpleasant. The culture of the people is merely superficial and *nobody* understands me. Besides this, I *cannot* reveal to anyone the purpose of my presence here. For this reason I live alone in a small house which I have rented for 3 months. I have fitted it with simple furnishings. I read the whole day. I have two colored servants. Although Indianapolis is situated in the same latitude as Palermo, Sicily, the climate here is colder than that of Northern Germany . . . .

. . . I am very hopeful of seeing you in Paris on June 9.

[*Original in English*][22]

TO J. H. SCHRODER, LONDON

Indianapolis, 15th May 1869

. . . In the long letter I wrote you end of December 1867 from Cuba I also discussed the case if the island were annexed to the U. S. Considering the gigantic filibustering expedition that are fitting out all along the Atlantic coast of the U. S., I have now no more any doubt that Cuba will be independent and annexed to the U. S. before the end of the present year, because Spain with its rotten finances and with the 11 P. C. it pays for money, can impossibly hold this island, where it has just as many enemies as there are inhabitants. And, when it comes to the U. S., as I explained to you in the aforesaid letter, though Slavery will thus at once be abolished, property will instantly double in value and you will see *great things going on there*. I think the present flourishing condition of our southern States, which were but 3 years ago covered with gore and anarchy, with ruins and wilderness and which by whole Europe were considered as lost to the commonwealth of this country for a century to come, cannot leave you the slightest doubt of the veracity of my words.

In fact, had I known a year ago that Cuba would so soon gravitate towards the U. S. I would never have sold my Cuban Bonds; but I saw then a storm coming and could not foresee what it would bring; I thought the island would still remain to Spain and slavery would merely be abolished, in which case our investment would have become depreciated for at least 5 years.

. . . The whole island of Cuba will, when annexed to the U. S. be in a 5 years time a vast and beautiful garden, crossed in all directions by well paying Railroads. . . .

[22] From Dr. Meyer, I, 148–49, by permission.

[Original in German][23]
TO HIS FATHER, ERNST SCHLIEMANN, SCHWERIN

Indianapolis,
May 18, 1869

. . . The Archbishop of Greece, my former teacher, has sent me the portraits of several Athenians for selection; I have chosen from these Sophia Engastromenos as the most lovable and it appears that the Archbishop, before he was promoted to the higher clergy and still thought of remaining a sinner, intended to marry her. At any rate I intend, if everything goes well, to go to Athens in July to marry her and with her to come to you, since as I am enthusiastic about the Greek language I believe that I can be happy only with a Greek. I will, however, take her only if she has a liking for sciences because I believe that a beautiful young girl can respect and love an old man only in the event she has enthusiasm for sciences in which he is much more advanced than she is. I have ordered 12 copies of Sophia's photograph and will send you one today or tomorrow. . . .

I know of several in Paris and Lyon who, after my departure, criticized my book ("Ithaka"); I do not know, however, how and in what papers, will learn later. Adolph Schliemann writes about it today from Schwerin: "I have already written you that your works have been highly praised by Professors Bachman and Fritsch in Rostock . . . and what has impressed everybody is the great spiritual strength with which you have worked and the goal you have achieved." . . .

[Original in English]
TO A. SEIDENSTICKER & CO., INDIANAPOLIS.

I undersigned U. S. Citizen do hereby certify that I have agreed with Messrs. A. Seidensticker & Co. and Mr. A. Nalkner to pay *to them conjointly* for the services they have rendered me and for those they have still to render me in my present divorce case, the sum of Fifteen Hundred dollars. But it is distinctly understood that this sum is due to them only in case I obtain my divorce in next month and that, in case I might not obtain my divorce in next month I have to pay to them, instead of said sum in all only two hundred dollars for their services.

Indianapolis, Ind. 20 May 1869 H. SCHLIEMANN

The above amount is to be paid by me *the moment* I receive from the Court the papers stating that my bonds of matrimony are dissolved.

H. SCHLIEMANN

[23] Translated by permission from Dr. Meyer, I, 149.

[Original in English][24]

TO [ABRAM W. HENDRICKS],[25] CONCERNING "THE THOUSAND AND ONE NIGHTS"

[Indianapolis,
from 20 to 23 May, 1869]

European writers, for the most part, pretend that the Arabian Nights were originally written in the Chinese language, though I have never been able to find out any proof for this supposition. In the chinese language most decidedly exist no Arabian Nights nor any similarly inter-woven 1001 tales. Had they been written in the Chinese language they would only have been written by a chinaman and all chinamen know more or less the geography of their empire. But wherever in the Arabian Nights the scene is in   [26](China) it appears beyond any doubt that the author had not even the faintest idea of chinese geography; he often calls China an island and he never gives the name of a chinese city that really exists or ever existed; even the etymology of all the chinese names of men or cities is pure arabian; *all* the manners and customs, laws and religion he describes are arabian. He speaks very often of the Eastindies but proves every where that he only know this country by name and even all his names of indian cities are fictitious. On the other all the names he gives of arabian cities are perfectly correct. Nearly all the tales pass in Bagdad and Bassora, but in a few instances also in   (Cairo) and   (Alexandria). The book was evidently written in the be-ginning of the 14th century, and, since Egypt belonged then to the Calif of Bagdad, the author has some notion of the geography of this country. In foreign countries he only mentions, with the right name, Theheran in Persia   and Constantinople (   ). In a few places he speaks of Christians but always with the profoundest contempt.

The opinion differ[s] regarding the author or translator of the Arabian Nights and I never saw yet an arabian edition with the author's name on the title-page. But my copy of this work is signed at the end in the fol-lowing manner:

[Arabic text here]   (Faharas has finished by the hand
of his scribe Elfakir
Hana Joseph may
god send him pardon
Amen   end)

By this it appears that Faharas or Fahras is called the author.

[24] From Dr. Meyer, I, 150–52, by permission.

[25] The index to Schliemann's copy press letter book for the year 1869 indicates that this dissertation on the Arabian Nights was addressed to Abram W. Hendricks. This was called to the editor's attention by Peter-Nick J. Vavalis.

[26] The blanks in this letter indicate places where Schliemann inserted words in Arabic script which have not been reproduced.

The author tells us that the origin of the Arabian Nights—in arabian which, litterally translated means one thousand and one nights—was as follows: Schacher Ras, king of the Chinese and the indian islands, having been deceived by the women of his harem, slew all of them and swore that he would never again have confidence in any woman, and that [he] would marry every day a fresh woman and kill her the following morning. He kept his oath for a long time killing every woman after she had been his wife for less than one day, so that at last no female wanted any more to marry him. At last   (Shaker Sad), the daughter of the Vizier, consented to become his wife. She knew that the king always killed his wifes at the first dawn of the morning and so she began one hour before daybreak to tell him a history and managed it so that when the king saw the dawn of the morning she was in the most interesting part of her story and said, now I stop in order to be beheaded but if the sultan likes my story and will delay killing me until to-morrow morning then I will tell him the end of it. She really told him the following morning the end of it but having terminated it she said that she knew another still far more interesting tale and when the dawn of the morning appeared she was again in the most beautiful part of it; the sultans curiosity was excited and he again delayed the execution for one day to hear the end of the story the following morning. In the same manner she continued for 1001 nights until at last the sultan lovestricken and full of wonder and admiration, swore not to kill her any more and not to take any more revenge on his new wifes for the infidelity of the former inmates of his harem.

The Arabian Nights are the greatest masterpiece of Arabian Litterature and it is quite inexplanable to me how the thought could ever occur that they might be a translation from the chinese. In fact the language is so genuine arabian and, except the [Alkoran] so far superior to all other arabian litterature and the poetry is so sublime and wonderful, that I defy any man to point out to me anything superior in the litterature of any other language. Strange to say the arabian language, which under[goes] so immense a change from the time of the great profet to the 12th century . . . how could already then, as it is now the case, . . . be understood by arabian scholars, the arabian language I say has undergone no change since the Arabian Nights were written and when travelling on the Nile I read the latter to my illiterate sailors they understood very well the prose of them.

More than one hundred of the Arabian tales are marvellous anecdotes of the great Chalif   (Haroun Elraschid), who reigned in Bagdad in the beginning of the 9th century, at the time of Charles the Great, and so it appears at first to the reader that the work must have been written shortly after the reign of that great monarch. But this is impossible because sciences and art began to flourish at Bassora and Bagdad 39 only in the beginning of the 10th century and the total transformation of the arabian language occurred in that and in the following centuries. If we compare the language of the arabian nights with works written in the 12th and the 13th century we find that they must have been written, as aforesaid, in the beginning of the 14th century.

Even in the very worst translation the Arabian Nights would be beautiful, but most unfortunately they are so full of infringements upon and violations of our arbitrary modern codex of conventional proprieties, they abound to such a degree with descriptions that would make the pandemonium blush that they cannot be translated as they are into the languages of civilized nations. Thus it happens that the existing translations, though disfigured, mutilated and hardly recognizable do not contain one fifth part of original 1001 arabian nights.

Certainly the language of the Alkoran is still far richer than that of the arabian nights, in fact one has sometimes to write a whole phrase in the language of the latter to render a single work of the Alkoran; but for centuries the language of the prophet had not been any more in use when the arabian nights were written. The Alkoran abounds to such a degree with beauties and sublime descriptions; its language is so marvelous by the shortness, conciseness, great and sonorous sound of the words, that even the Christian scholar, in reading it, risks to become fanatic of it and to believe in the veracity of the chapter. . . .

[Original in French][27]

TO TH. THIBAUT-BRIGNOLLES,[28] ST. PETERSBURG

Indianapolis,
May 23, 1869

. . . I was at first very surprised to read in your letter that general Stuart, your son's supposed father-in-law, was a small Southern land-

[27] Translated by permission from Dr. Meyer, I, 152–53.

[28] A number of the letters which Henry Schliemann wrote from Indianapolis concern his endeavors to find the whereabouts of Edward Thibaut-Brignolles, the son of Th. Thibaut-Brignolles. Schliemann had known the father in St. Petersburg. According to the letters the son had emigrated to America in 1863, had entered the Union army, and in 1864 married Margaret (Maggie) Stewart (or Stuart), the daughter of a Confederate General Stewart. The son was supposed to have fought in almost all the battles waged under the command of General Sherman. His father had not received any news from him for the last three years and did not know where he was. The last letter which he sent to his father, in March, 1866, from Williamsburg, New York, said that he had retired from the service in 1865 with the rank of captain. He also mentioned that he intended to go to Memphis to visit his father-in-law and brother-in-law. Schliemann sent letters of inquiry to General Beauregard, Charles Parsons of St. Louis, Colonel John S. Preston, of Lexington, Virginia, Charles Rhodes, of Oswego, New York, General Alexander P. Stewart, John D. Stewart and L. H. Stewart, of Memphis, Tennessee, and made trips to Memphis and St. Louis. He also inserted an advertisement, offering a $50.00 reward for information

owner before the war and that his daughter was compelled to go to New York and to get a job in order to earn a living. But all this is impossible, for in this country where the only aristocracy is that of wealth it is necessary, in order to become a general, or even only a colonel, to have gone through the great military school of West Point and to have passed all the courses; a candidate for the rank of general must also equip, at his own expense, a battalion of soldiers; a candidate for the grade of colonel must equip a corps at his expenses, following which they make an offer to the government, submitting the certificates from said military school and offering their services for said ranks. Thus, in addition to military capabilities, two things are essential in getting to these high ranks; first, a man must be *very popular* and highly respected in the state where he lives, as otherwise volunteers certainly could not be found . . . and he must have a huge fortune in order to be able to equip a battalion or just a corps of soldiers and to support it for several months as it takes at least two months to train the recruits. . . .

[*Original in English*][29]

TO DR. H. DRISLER, NEW YORK

Indianapolis, Ind.,
29 May 1869

For the Convention of American Philologists, to be held in Poughkeepsi, New York, commencing on Tuesday 27 July 1869.[30]

To the question: "How much time in a Collegiate course of study should be given to the study of Language" I answer as Charles V justly observed to Francis I: "every new language on[e] acquires is a new life" for by the knowledge of the language of a foreign country we are able to get acquainted with its literature; of which in most cases no translation

on Edward Thibaut-Brignolles, in newspapers published in New York City and Albany, New York; Pittsburgh and Philadelphia, Pennsylvania; Memphis, Tennessee, Richmond, Virginia, and New Orleans. Presumably the young man was never located.

[29] From Dr. Meyer, I, 153-57, by permission.

[30] In the Proceedings of the Convention of the American Philologists at Poughkeepsie, New York, in July, 1869, it is recorded that at the morning session of July 29, "Doctor Crosby read a paper by Doctor Schliemann of Paris, in which it was urged that at least one half of the time of the collegiate course should be devoted to the study of language, and that but a single language, in addition to the student's mother tongue, should be studied at a time. Dr. Schliemann also recommended that a chair of American Indian languages be added to the faculties of our universities." At the same meeting the American Philological Association voted thanks to Dr. Schliemann for a copy of the *Transactions* of the Association pour l'Encouragement des Études Grecques. These Proceedings are printed in the *Transactions* of the American Philological Association, 1869–70 (Hartford, Conn., 1871). See pp. 18–19 for above quotation. There is a letter in the Schliemann papers from George F. Comfort, secretary, American Philological Association, May 23, 1870, to Schliemann, in which he says that he is sending two copies of these Proceedings to him.

exists, and if it exists it can never give us more than a faint idea of the beauties of the original. Besides the knowledge of the language of a foreign nation enables us to study with great precision their manners and customs, and to gather a vast deal of useful information, which we can otherwise only collect imperfectly and incorrectly. I am therefore of opinion that one half of the time should be devoted to the study of language. To the following questions, from 2 to 7, I reply: the great drawback in the schools are usually that the pupils are overworked, and that they study too many languages at once, for man's head is like man's stomach, and in the same manner as the stomach, which is continually overloaded with a great variety of dishes will fall into incurable chronical dyspepsy, in the same manner the man's head which is continually overstrained by the study of too many languages at once, falls into an incurable chronical confusion which will forever impede him to learn any one language thoroughly. Any man who has a taste for languages will be able to perform wonders if he devotes his principal attention to only one language at a time and if he pursue the right method which is to read much aloud, never to make translations, to write always dissertations on subjects that interest us, to correct them under the eye of the teacher, to commit them to memory and to repeat them word by word in the lesson of the following day. By this method and owing to the similitude of the german language with the english, an american boy, who is only taught in private lessons, would master in a 6 months time the difficulties of the german language, viz. he would be able to speak and write it correctly.

In the College this method has of course to be modified, but even in its modified form it is bound to procure wonderful results. I am therefore of opinion that there should be in all classes only 5 lessons daily and that out of the 30 weekly lessons 15 should be devoted to the study of language. In the lowest class, Quarta, there should be weekly 3 english and 12 german lessons. The smart pupils will certainly not require more than 1 year to speak and to write the german language *correctly* by studying it in Quarta in the aforesaid method, though in its modified form and therefore in the following class, Tertia, there should be only one german and one english weekly lessons whilst 13 hours a week should be devoted to the study of the french language. However difficult the latter may be to the anglosaxon descendents, in commencing it in Tertia, they have the great advantage that they know of proximately 4000 german words, by the learning of which they have strengthened their memory and got the knack at studying. Thus . . . they will no more find any difficulty to render themselves in another year masters of the french language.

In Secunda the french should be kept up by two lessons a week and german and english should be continued by one weekly lesson each, whilst 10 hours weekly should be devoted to the study of the *modern* greek language under a native greek teacher. In beginning this new language the pupils have already a thorough knowledge of the english, german and french languages—they know at least 8000 foreign words and their memory is fortified in such a manner, that, by following the aforedescribed method, they most easily learn to write and to converse correctly in modern greek in less than a year. In fact it did not require me in St. Petersburg, Russia, more than 6 weeks to speak and to write this language with fluency; but I acquired it by privat lessons and at the age of 34.

In Prima should be two divisions and ancient greek ought to be commenced in *lower* Prima by 12 weekly lessons, where english, german, french and modern greek should there be represented each by only one lesson a week. The knowledge of the modern greek language wonderfully facilitates the study of classical greek, for at least a thousand words are in both languages identical; perhaps another thousand words show but a slight difference and the *accent* which renders the ancient greek so enormously difficult to those who do not know the modern idiom is in both . . . the same. The afore explained method is also capital for the learning of the classical greek, although it must be still more modified regarding the written exercises owing to the difficulty for the teacher to correct them. Two lessons weekly should be given to the greek grammar, which may be gone through 3 or 4 times in one year, but it must be done in a more cursory and by no means in too pedantic way, for every pupil will learn the grammar far better by the practical explanation of the classical authors than by the tiresome theoretical comments on the grammar. Since the principal object of greek studies is always to understand the classical authors 6 lessons weekly should be allotted to comment the ancient masterpieces of literature. The remaining 4 greek lessons may be employed to correct the pupils exercises and to let them recite corrected in the previous lessons.

Regarding the comment of the classical greek books I must remark, that, since the pupils must always be prepared for what is likely to be read and commented in the lesson and since they must have learnt the words by heart, it is very obnoxious indeed to proceed too slowly, for that would fatigue the pupil without benefitting him; in order to keep his greatest curiosity always awake, not less for example than 100 verses of Homer, Sophocles, Aristophanes or Pindar should be explained in a lesson.

The laborious pupil who has gone through the classes with the method aforeindicated, will not have the slightest difficulty to make himself in lower Prima in a 12 months' time sufficiently master of classical greek to write fluently a tolerably good dissertation and to translate—unprepared —any one of the classical greek authors (except Lycophron's Alexandra or Cassandra) into english, german, french and modern greek. 43

Latin should never be commenced before the pupil reaches Upper-Prima, because just as enormously difficult as it is to learn ancient greek, if one knows only a little latin, just as enormously easy is it to learn latin if one knows modern and ancient greek, french, english and german.

Since there is no philological faculty in any one of the U[nited] St[ates] universities, I think that in Upper-Prima, out of the 30 weekly lessons, 22 ought to be given to the study of 6 Language, viz.: 1 english, 1 german, 1 french, 1 modern greek, 6 ancient greek an[d] 12 latin. In latin the same method, as applied to the ancient greek, will enable the assiduous pupil—who already knows 4 living languages, who has the great advantage of possessing the classical greek and who thus has at least 20,000 foreign words in his head—not only to understand every author, but also to speak and to write the language (the latin) correctly in a 12 months' time.

If the Collegiate course of instruction were arranged in this manner and if the afore described method were adopted, then the result would be vastly different of what it is now. Now the poor fellows sit 8 and 10 years in the colleges and *never* bring it so far as to have but a superficial knowledge of any foreign language and their accomplishment in greek and latin are so slight, so insignificant, that a year after having left College, *no* man can understand Ovid or Virgil, Homer or Euripides and far less Horace, Sophocles or Pindar.

If the change were introduced as I propose it, the boy, who enters Quarta at the age of eleven, would be able to leave College at the age of 16 with a thorough knowledge of 6 languages and these 6 languages having been acquired in succession and the most difficult ones having always been founded as it were upon the firm basis of a thoroughly mastered modern language of the same root, *nothing* can ever be lost, because man can *only* forget the language of which he has but a superficial knowledge, but *never* can he forget a language which he has once completely mastered and thoroughly known.

Certainly the written accent should be observed in pronouncing classical greek, because, since in modern greek, which entirely derives from ancient greek, the accent is always observed with the greatest precision, there cannot be the slightest doubt such has also been the case in ancient times. I ask for what purpose the accent can possibly [have] been used if not for making the pronounciation.

The german pronounciation of the latin should be adopted, for it is the only right one: the spelling of latin words by classical greek authors leave no doubt in this respect. I must however [except?] the letter C, which has evidently been pronounced by the Romans as K as is known by the greek spelling of Cicero's name as Κικέρων.

It is probable that in the classical antiquity there was some difference
44   in the sound of *oi*, η, υ, ει, υε and ι and there can be no doubt that B

was pronounced as the english b, for if it had sounded as the english v, as in fact it does in modern greek, the classics would have written Βιργίλιος and not Ουϊργίλιος as they do. But most probably already as far back as the 5th century after Christ the ancient greek was pronounced perfectly so as is now pronounced the modern greek; at all events we have certain proofs that this was the case in the 11th century, because all the greek words, which then passed into the russian language by the adoption of the greek religion in Russia have in the russian language eminently the modern greek pronounciation. We find a further proof of it in a symbol of the Faith of the early part of the 13th century, conserved in this greek manuscript No. 2408 of the Imperial Library at Paris, page 223, where the greek text is accompanied by a translation in ancient french or degenerated latin, written in greek characters, the cop[y]ist having evidently gone to great trouble to render the pronounciation by the greek alphabet. He renders the sound of the latin i sometimes by οι or η, at others by υ, ει or ι; the sound of the latin d he always renders by ντ. It is therefore my advice that Erasmian or Universitary pronounciation of the classical greek, which is at all events false and erroneous, should be condemned and rejected and that the modern greek pronounciation should at once be introduced.

. . . I should be most happy to see that the changes I propose were introduced into the colleges, for the new system cannot fail to create and to develop in the intelligent american public the hitherto unknown and therefore unfelt passion for the most noble and most charming of sciences.

Until now the Americans have always been looked upon in Europe as perfectly incapable for philological studies and even incapable to acquire a thorough knowledge of any foreign language whatever. But I know that this deficing [deficiency] merely arises from their most miserable system in the Colleges, and I am perfectly certain, that, if the new system I propose were introduced, this great nation would, in twenty years hence, take the lead of all european nations in philological pursuits and that american genius would perform in philological studies and discoveries just as great wonders as it had until now performed in material arts and in gigantic enterprises.   HENRY SCHLIEMANN

[*Original in English*]
TO L. VON HOFFMANN, NEW YORK

Indianapolis,
5 June 1869

My dear Sir,

I have to-day a great request to make you by granting which, you would bind me to everlasting gratitude.

You know that I have here a Lawsuit of a serious nature and though I feel confident that by the aid of the honorable attorneys, to whom I was introduced here by your kind intercession, I shall win the case, yet this might be rendered to them much easier if I could prove that I hold property in this country. Unfortunately all my U. S. 5/20 Bonds are with Messrs. J. [illeg.] Co. and besides they are *not* registered. But all my Railway shares, of which you hold my full powers, stand in my name in the books of the Companies.

May I therefore beg you to apply, on *the very day* you receive this letter, to the Illinois Central in which I hold 216 shares, to the Michigan Central in which I have 220 sh, to the Chicago Burlington and Quincy in which I have 62 sh and to the Cleveland & Toledo in which, if you received the last dividend, I have 110 sh and require from them a little certificate, with the stamp of the companies, stating merely that in their books figure so and so many shares to the name of Henry Schliemann. But pray explain distinctly to them that *nothing* more is required and that they must by *no means* add my place of residence (Paris and the street and number) as it stands in their books. But this can easily be avoided if you state the facts, viz: that I reside for the present in the U. S. and finding it useful to prove in a suit that I hold property in this country, I require said certificates without statement of my residence. This of course they will wilfully do at *your* request.

Perhaps one or two of the Companies are in Boston and in that case please get me and send me *at once* the certificates of those which are in N. Y. and the other a day or two later.

I beg you a thousand pardons for troubling you so much and assure you that nothing will give me more pleasure than to serve you in return. I remain with sincere regard my dear sir yours truthfully

H. SCHLIEMANN

L. VON HOFFMANN ESQ.[31]

[31] L. von Hoffmann & Co., New York, served as Schliemann's agent and banking house. It paid to him while he was in Indianapolis, through the First National Bank of Indianapolis, $4,800, made up as follows: April 10, $500; May 1, $300; May 20, $1000; May 31, $500; June 7, $500; June 21, $1000, and June 24, $1000. E. Erlanger & Co., of Paris, remitted to him on June 24, 1869, 1,000 French francs. Doubtless he received other payments from these and other banks during this period, but it would be an impossible task to examine the voluminous Schliemann papers to confirm this assumption. Other businesses and banks with which he had dealings while in Indianapolis include: Chicago Rail Road Company, J. N. Denison, president; Illinois Central Rail Road Company; Chicago Burlington and Quincy Railroad Company, J. N. Denison, chairman; Lake Shore Railway Company, Cleveland, George B. Ely, president; MacKillop, Sprague & Company, New York; Farmers Loan and Trust Company, New York, R. C. Rolston, president; Janssen, Schmidt & Rupert, New York.

[*Original in English*]
TO E. W. SCHLIEMANN, BORDEAUX

Indianapolis,
6 June 1869

My dear brother

I last wrote to you on 19th ult. and received since your letters of 4 and 19th, from which I am happy to see that you give the pleasure of your visit at Paris on my return from the far West. I had already engaged passage on board the steamer of the 26th inst., but have written yesterday to New York to transfer my ticket from that date to the steamer of 10th July, for I can not well leave this city so soon as I expected. The court sits from the 7th inst. until the 19th July and I cannot press my suit without raising suspicion. I think nevertheless that it will come forth by the 16th or 18th inst.; I certainly hope to win it, but it would look badly if I start at once as soon as I get my decree. . . .

I shall telegraph you from Brest and should be glad if you could make it possible to arrive with me in Paris [or] ab't 2 days after me, for I shall have there plenty of work for some days. I think to leave Paris on Thursday 29th July for Athens. Enclosed is a photograph of Sophie Engastromenos; since I have never yet seen her I cannot judge whether she will please me or not. If I marry a greek woman she may perhaps have a sister to suit you. . . .   H. SCHLIEMANN

[*Original in Greek*]

Indianapolis,
8 June 1869

Most Honorable Mr. Egger!

. . . Europeans to this day have considered Americans utterly incapable of philosophical pursuits, and of learning any foreign language thoroughly. However, I know that the wretched methods employed in high schools are solely responsible for this failing. Should new methods be introduced, I am convinced this great nation would in 20 years be second to none in philological studies and that American genius would accomplish in scholarship and philological research miracles equal to those it has already produced in the physical sciences and in *gigantic business enterprises*.

I am trying to get my divorce as an *American citizen*. Everything here is decided by law. In the eyes of the law a marriage is a civil contract, which no longer exists when broken by one party or the other. My marriage has long since been broken by my wife. This I prove by her letters,[32] and so I hope to gain my freedom soon.

[32] These letters are given below, pp. 65–68.

[*Original in Greek*]

Indianapolis, 20 June 1869

Most Honorable Mr. Egger!

I shall attend the meeting of American philologists . . . about the end of July (27) in New York and then I hope to be in Paris on August 19. . . .

The temperature changes here are very sudden. Although 8 days ago it was cold . . . and it was necessary to light heaters, and . . . [put on] winter clothes, in a few days a heat wave caused the temperature to rise to 39°C [93°F] in the shade. On account of the humidity, the heat is unbearable and oppressive. Since the city is surrounded by swamps, the heat causes pestilential infections. At least one third of the population is afflicted with fevers. As a prophylactic measure, every morning I take a little quinine which I trust grants me immunity.

[*Original in Greek*]

Washington in America, [Indianapolis]
30 June 1869

. . . Friend Antonios Amiras!

. . . The wise lawmakers of the United States consider marriage a legal contract, which no longer exists if broken by one or the other of the contracting parties. Thus after 3 months' anticipation, my divorce was declared today . . . with Katerina Petrovna . . .

. . . I believe, my friend, that I can offer you no better proof of my Philhellenism than this: I forsake American women, the most beautiful women of the world . . . and I go to the far lands of the East to find a Greek wife . . . .

[*Original in Greek*]

Indianapolis, 1 July 1869

TO E. EGGER, PARIS
Most Honorable Friend!

. . . Today, finally, the court here granted me my divorce. Therefore, with the help of the gods I shall leave New York on August 7 . . .

[*Original in Greek*]

Indianapolis, 1 July 1869

TO ARCHBISHOP THEOKLETOS VIMBOS, ATHENS
Most Honorable Friend—

The local court has just granted my divorce *today*. Therefore with
48   the help of God I shall leave New York August 7 for France, and on

August 28 from Marseilles for Athens. . . . Thus I hope on September 4 to be in the fatherland of gods and heroes. From this country I shall most certainly take a wife, but I don't know whom—perhaps Sophia, or Polyxena, or some other.

Now I can tell you that I am in every respect most fit to marry a Greek wife.

So until we meet, Your friend HENRY SCHLIEMANN

[*Original in English*]

Indianapolis,
11 July 1869

MESSRS. A. SEIDENSTICKER & CO. PRESENT

Dear Sir:

I beg leave to inform you that I intend going to New York and that I shall be back here in the beginning of August.

But to provide for the contingency that I might be detained there by my business transactions, I beg you to take note that my rent on the house at No. 22 North Noble St. of $16.66 (Sixteen dollars sixty six Cents) is payable to Mr. English on the 6th of each month. Thus, for the months from the 6th of August until the 6th December same would amount to $66.64

In the same lapse of time you will receive for rent of my house No. 471 [South] Illinois Street at $10 pr m'th $40—

off your commission 10 pr ct 4— 36.—
30.64

which I hand you herewith, begging you to make the payment to Mr. English when due.

I am Dear Sir yours respectfully

H. SCHLIEMANN

[*Original in Greek*]

Indianapolis,
11 July 1869

Most Highly Honored Friend Mr. Egger!

. . . The court has issued my divorce. To achieve this end I bought a house here with a garden for $1,125 . . .[33] And in addition, I bought for $12,000 (or about Fr. 50,000) a one-third share in a large starch factory established here, with the agreement that I pay $350 (Fr. 1400) in cash, and the remainder on July 25. If I don't pay the remaining sum by that date, then the agreement is canceled and the seller will make no

[33]See above, p. 21.

claim beyond the $350 already paid.[34] On the day my case was being heard, I brought into court these two men, one of whom swore that I had purchased a house from him, the other that I had purchased from him a one third share in his starch factory. Both men took true oaths.

Since only a person who intends to reside *permanently* in a city will buy property and factories, the court believed this to be my intention too. So the court did not delay in granting me a divorce on the basis of my former wife's letters in which she refuses to live with me anywhere except in Russia. According to the laws of this country, a decision of the court concerning divorce is irrevocably inviolable and infrangible.

. . . Naturally I have now canceled my purchase of the starch factory, but I shall always retain the house, which brings an annual income of $120 (Fr. 480).

The court's recess begins the evening of the 14th, and all the decisions of this session concerning divorce become then irrevocable. For this reason I have decided to leave from here the morning of July 15.

. . . In any case I shall remain in New York two weeks.

. . . The increase in population is above all due to the perpetual, large immigration from Europe, which annually comes to more than 600,000 souls.

The Germans are particularly respected here because of their good sense, industry, steadiness, competence, kindliness, and honesty.

There is here a horrible and odd inclination to suicide. All the newspapers are always full of news of suicides. In spite of the fact that Americans are, generally speaking, a great and most splendid people, and that there is found here a kindness and honesty not to be found in any country of the Old World, still there exist here much greater and many more criminals than in any country of Europe. Every day all the newspapers are full of stories of murders and robberies of unbelievable size. The police are a disgrace and the more able officers of the police always participate in the big robberies. For example, a few days ago some enterprising rogues broke into one of New York's largest banks, opened all the great combination locks of the safes, hitherto considered unbreakable works of Hephaistos, and stole many millions. In Paris such a robbery would be impossible, because the much-feared officers of the French police would have caught them in the very act, or at least on the same day. But in America no one believes that the robbers of this bank will be apprehended, even though a reward of Fr. 100,000 has been offered for their capture.

. . . I begin to doubt whether I shall find a berth on the steamship leaving on the 24th. Because of the excessive heat and the prevalence of cholera and other diseases, many are fleeing from New York and the

50   [34]See above, pp. 21–22.

ships are crowded with passengers. Should I be compelled to wait for the boat of August 7, then naturally I shall go to the philologists' convention, which begins on July 27 . . .

[Original in English][35]

TO CHARLES PARSONS,[36] ST. LOUIS

Indianapolis, Ind.,
16 [July] 1869

I duly received your esteemed favor of 7th inst. as also Mr. Silas Bent's[37] address upon the Thermometric Gateways to the Pole, which I have read with *immense* interest. If you have a taste for scientific pursuits, as for instance the Northpolequestion then I garanty to you that you can never feel tedious if you make Paris your home. The opinion emitted by said Mr. Bent perfectly agree with those of Mr. Lambert[38] of the Polytechnical institution of Paris, who has raised some funds by public subscription, had bought a vessel and was going to start for the North-pole by way of the Behring's-Straits. But the amount he collected falls short of 200,000 francs, whereas, in my opinion, at least three times as much is required to do the thing well. Unfortunately, inspite of his profound knowledge, he has not had tact of enough to insinuate himself with the french minister of the Marine, who considers him a visionary man and refuses therefore all an[d] every assistance on the part of the french gouvernement. The emperor gave him 50000 francs from his private purse and nearly the whole rest of the money he has got was subscribed by us members of the parisian geographical society. Though the route

[35] From Dr. Meyer, I, 158–59, by permission.

[36] Charles Parsons (b. 1824), St. Louis financier. He was born and educated in Cortland County, New York, and came west to Keokuk, Iowa, in 1851. During the Civil War he had charge of army transportation in St. Louis, with rank of captain. In 1870 he became president of the State National Bank in St. Louis. He was also president of the St. Louis Clearing House and president of the American Bankers Association. *National Cyclopædia of American Biography*, XII (1904), 424.

[37] Silas Bent (1820–1887), native of St. Louis, a naval officer and oceanographer. "The Thermometric Gateways to the Pole" was an address before the St. Louis Historical Society in 1868, printed in St. Louis the following year. "In this and in a later publication (1872) he maintained that the Gulf Stream from the Atlantic and the Kuro Siwo from the Pacific maintained an open sea about the North Pole. At this time considerable interest in the North Pole exploration was manifested both in Europe and America and while Bent's conclusions with regard to an open Polar Sea were not accepted by the leading authorities, his theses encouraged discussion of the problems of polar exploration." *Dictionary of American Biography*, II (1929), 206.

[38] Gustave Lambert, French oceanographer, who drew a map of the Bering Strait in 1864. He believed that an open sea lay to the north of the Strait by which the North Pole could be reached. He raised by public subscription funds for a polar expedition which was forestalled by the Franco-Prussian War. *La Grande Encyclopédia* (31 volumes. Paris, 1886–1902), XXI, 821.

this expedition takes is in my opinion the only one by which men can ever succeed to get to the Northpole and though Mr. Lambert is no doubt the most clever man that ever tried to clear up the mysteries of the arctic world, yet his attempts will be frustrated on the very beginning for want of the most necessary and his expedition is therefore of *no* account.

But if such a scheme fails in France, where 999 out of 1000 have more taste to see "Hamlet" than they have to know the exact statistics of the Pole, it could not possibly fail in the U. S., where useful knowledge goes beyond every other consideration and where every one seems to be born with a passion for geography. The only thing would be to start the thing in a serious manner and to get some great american geographer at the head; I would joyfully contribute myself. Please speak with Mr. Silas Bent how such an expedition might best be got up in this our great country, which is more entitled than any other to the glory to have reached the Pole. Pray, ask Mr. S. Bent also by what arctic exploration our fellow-citizen Dr. Isaac I. Hayes[39] has gained this years great golden medal of the parisian geographical society? I saw a notice of it the other day in the paper, but I do not know of any recent expedition of Dr. Hayes. . . .

[*Original in English*]

New York,
20th July 1869

My dear Mr. Naltner
I have spoken here with Messrs. L. von Hoffmann and other Bankers, also with my old friends Messrs. Janssen, Schmidt & Rupert, and several money brokers regarding the business you propose, but unfortunately [the] sum is quite out of the question in the present state of the money-market here. In fact although money is again plenty on call at 7 pr ct., it easily fetches 12 per ct on very prime signatures, for short terms, whilst on long terms no loans can be made at any rate. The reason is the wild speculation in stocks. He who has the opportunity can often make here as much as [?] pr ct per day for money. I am exceedingly sorry that I cannot be useful to you here. In Europe I neither have any chance to get you a loan, because my friends there, who are in the habit of lending money on mortgages, only make those operations in the very city in which they reside and never out of the country.

[39] Isaac Israel Hayes (1832–1881) physician and explorer. He was a member of Elisha Kent Kane's second Arctic expedition as surgeon, 1853-55, and organized his own expedition of 1860–61. Despite certain erroneous conclusions which he drew, he, along with Kane and Charles Francis Hall, opened the way to the North Pole. He published *Open Polar Sea* (1867) and an account of his adventures for children, *Cast Away in the Cold* (1868). *Dictionary of American Biography*, VIII (1932), 445–46.

It is probable that my business transactions will retain me here until the middle of August and that I shall not be able to return to Indianapolis before 20th August

. . .

In thanking you some more for all the kindness and friendship you have shown me during my stay at Indianapolis I remain with cordial greetings and hearty wishes for you and your dear family's constant good health and good luck, your friend   H. SCHLIEMANN

[*Original in English*]   Paris,
19 August 1869
6 Place St. Michel

TO THE COURT OF COMMON PLEAS IN THE CITY HALL IN NEW YORK

In a lawsuit which I have pending here I require a copy of the declaration I made in New York on the 17th February 1851 to become a citizen of the United States of America. I therefore solicit the Court to let me have said copy with the Court seal affixed to it.

I further beg leave to solicit the Court to let me have through the bearer hereof a copy of the declaration and renunciation I made on the 29th March 1869 in taking out my second papers as Citizen of the United States of America.[40]

I beg the Court will let me have the above two copies on two separate pieces of paper and remain respectfully,   HENRY SCHLIEMANN

[*Original in English*]   New York,
1 September 1869[41]

A NALTNER ESQ. INDIANAPOLIS

My dear Sir!

I expected to be back in Indianapolis by this time but to my greatest regret I am detained here by some business which will probably delay my return until the end of this month.

[40] It is interesting to note that Schliemann, in his Autobiography, wrote, "Happening, therefore, to be in California when, on the 4th of July, 1850, it was made a State, and all those there resident in the country became by that very fact naturalized Americans, I joyfully embraced the opportunity of becoming a citizen of the United States." Schliemann, *Ilios*, p. 12. Schliemann's usual fine memory played him false, for as the above letter indicates, he applied for his first citizenship papers in New York on February 17, 1851, on his way to California. He was not in California on July 4, 1850, and furthermore, California was not made a state until September 9, 1850. He did not attain his citizenship until March 29, 1869. The dates of his declaration of intent and naturalization have been confirmed by the Immigration and Naturalization service of the U. S. Department of Justice.

[41] This letter is of interest because on the day it is dated, September 1, 1869, Schliemann was in Athens, not in New York. Presumably he sent the letter to New York, probably to his agent L. von Hoffmann & Co., requesting that it be transmitted to Mr. Naltner.

Pray, present my respects to the Honorable Hendricks as also to his respected partners and believe me to remain,

My dear Sir, yours faithfully

H. SCHLIEMANN

[Original in German]   Athens,
                                                September 21, 1869

My dear Mr. Naltner!

For some time I have not had the pleasure of hearing from you but I hope that you and your wonderful wife are all right.

I have been here for 3 weeks to choose a wife out of this land of buoyancy. The first lawyers in Germany consider my divorce legal and claim that it is legal throughout the world. All these lawyers have the same opinion. Because being continuously alone has tormented me tremendously, I do not want to wait for remarriage much longer. My former wife has expressed her extreme satisfaction with the divorce as long as I continue to provide for her and the children.

Therefore, nothing can ever be done against me by Catherine Schliemann, either in Indianapolis where I obtained my divorce or in Athens where I am getting married the day after tomorrow to Sophia Engastromenos, or in Paris where I live.

You know my Sophia because you liked her picture best of the 3 pictures which I had with me in Indianapolis. I sign all documents as an inhabitant of Indianapolis. Do you think it would be right if I come back soon? . . .

[Original in German]   Paris,
                                                2 Decb. 1869
                                                6 Place St. Michel

My dear friend Naltner!

Herewith I acknowledge my . . . letter of November 2, in which I wrote you that I do not want to keep my house on my account for Mr. English longer than December 5; that I am giving as a present to Mr. Lorenz Schmidt[42] the rent to be collected from my house on Illinois Street from November 28 to March 28, that is, thirty-six dollars for six months; and that I ask you as of March 28 to put the rent from my house to my account regularly and to credit me also for the net amount of the . . . [illeg.] deposited by Mr. English, which you should sell at the best possible time, with the latest time being April 1, 1870.

In the meantime, I received your dear letter of November 6 and I

[42] Lorenz Schmidt, listed in the Indianapolis *Directory* for 1869, as clerk for A. Seidensticker & Co.

54

thank you very much for the good wishes and greetings from you and your dear family.

In answer to your question, I wish to tell you, without taking any responsibility, that Mr. Müller is not only a great man of honor but also a smart and excellent businessman. I had a hundred occasions to find these qualities in you, *and therefore I am sure* that the business you two are starting together has to have excellent results, if you are cautious and if the purchasing and selling takes place right there.[43] However, if you, as I suspect, want to sell the products of your factory to New York . . . [illeg.] to trust the merchandise.

I advise you especially to establish such a business for yourself and your dear son, where everything is under your control at all the times. With your knowledge and energy you should sweep away any competition and nobody could compete with you. If large quantities have to be sent to the seashore, you have to depend on the sincerity of your agents and you often lose out.

I would not like to be part of a business which I could not see at all times, and, therefore, I cannot accept your kind offer. Besides, I have been away from active business for so many years, that I do not have enough capacity or interest. . . .

Maybe next spring I can come with my wife to Indianapolis but as yet I cannot say for sure.

With many hearty greetings . . .

HY. SCHLIEMANN

[Auction of Schliemann's Household Articles]

This is to certify that I received of Aegidius Naltner the following Goods to be sold on public Auction, to wit—

1 Bedstead with springs, Mattress & Pillows—1 Bed tick—2 Bed Sheets & Pillow slips—1 Sofa Lounge—1 Table—1 Kitchen Table & Window Curtains—1 Wash stand—1 Cooking stove and pipe—1 Water Kettle—1 Copper Kettle—1 Oil Can—1 Small Shovel—1 Ladle—1 Tin Water Bucket—1 Wash Bowl & Pitcher—4 Pans/Bread & others/—1 Small Grater—1 Wash Board—½ Doz. Clothes Pins—10 Common Chairs—1 Bureau with looking Glass—1 Carpet—1 Tin Wash Boiler—1 Coffee Mill—4 China plates, 3 Coffee Cups & 2 saucers—1 Caster with 4 Cruets—3 spoons—3 knifes & 2 teaspoons—6 Water Glasses—1 Waiter—1 Sugar Bowl—2 Oval Dishes—2 . . . pots—1 Kitchen Safe—1 Cake [stands] . . .

Indianapolis—Nov. 29, 1869

M. DELLEFIELD.
AUCTIONEER

[43] On November 6, 1869, Naltner wrote to Schliemann that Edward Mueller had sold his share of the Union Starch Factory (see above, p. 22n) to the other partners; and that Mueller and he (Naltner) were opening their own starch works on the other side of town. They asked Schliemann to become a partner in their enterprise. Naltner's letter is in the Schliemann papers.

The following Articles of Household furniture sold at Public Auction by Rothschild & Co. for the following prices.[44]

1 Bedstead with springs,			$ 6.70
Mattress & Pillow	$1.95	1 Small Grater	.04
1 Bed Tick	.20	1 Wash Board	.15
2 Sheets	.60	½ Clothes Pins	.02
1 Wash Tub	.30	2 Common Chairs	.50
4 Pillow Slips	.25	8 Common Chairs	2.00
1 Sofa Lounge	.75	1 Bureau & Glass	2.85
1 Table	.35	1 Carpet	.50
1 Kitchen Table	.80	1 Tin Wash Bowl	.20
3 Window Curtains	.50	1 Coffee Mill	.10
1 Wash Stand	.30	4 Plates, Cups & Saucers	.15
1 Water Kettle	.05	1 Caster/4 Kruets	.10
1 Copper Kettle	.10	3 spoons, 3 knives &	
		3 teaspoons	.15
1 Oil Can	.05	6 Water Glasses	.10
1 Small shovel	.05	1 Waiter, 1 sugar bowl	.10
1 Ladle	.05	2 Oval dishes	.10
1 Tin Water Bucket	.05	1 Kitchen Safe	.75
1 Wash Bowl & Pitcher	.25	2 Pots & 2 cake stds.	.10
4 Pans, bread and others	.10	1 Cooking Stove & Pipe	3.05
	$6.70		17.66
		Less Commission	1.75
		Bal. Due	$15.91

by M. S. DELLEFIELD

[44] Aegidius Naltner wrote to Schliemann on December 12, 1869, as follows: "I received your letter of November 2 and immediately talked with L. Schmidt about your things in the house, but he said most of them were gone with the black people who were at your place. However, he made a list of everything and sent it to you. I . . . gave the resulting money [from the auction] to the Seidensticker & Co., but it was very little. I send you herewith the entire bill and your ballance after settling . . . everything. As soon as you want the money, you can draw from the firm for the sum. . . ."

Schliemann was not happy with the results of the sale. He wrote to Naltner in an undated letter, ". . . and the big kitchen stove with pipes and all accessories for which I paid $21.—is sold for $3.—! I have never seen such a 'wonderful' sale!" In his Diary Schliemann wrote that he spent about $200 furnishing his house. See above, p. 14.

1869					1869				
July	26	To cash pd Mary Brooks	$ 5	00	July	12	By Cash of Hy Schliemann	$ 30	64
"	29	" Com	1	00	"	23	" "		5 00
Aug.	6	" Rent pd Wm. H. English	16	66	"	29	" Rent of Bolser	10	00
"	30	" Com.	1	00	Aug.	30	" "	10	00
Sept.	7	" Rent pd Wm. H. English	16	66	Sept.	29	" "	10	00
"	29	" Com.	1	00	Oct.	30	" "	10	00
Oct.	9	" Rent pd Wm. H. English	16	66	Dec.	1	" "	10	00
Oct.	13	" Insurance pd for house on South Illinois Street	4	50	"	1	" Cash of Rothchild & Co. auctioneers by M. S. Dellefield for furniture and other household		
"	30	" Com.	1	00			goods	17	65
Nov.		Amount carried over	$ 63	48			Amt. carried over	$103	29
Nov.	6	To Rent till Dec. 6th'69 pd Wm. H. English	16	66					
"	29	" Cash pd Expressman for hauling Household Goods to Auction room		75					
Dec.	1	" Com. pd Rothchild & Co. for sale of household goods	1	75					
"	1	" Com. on rent	1	00					
"	1	" Cash pd L. Schmidt	9	00					
"	1	" Balance credited to new a/c	10	65					
			$103	29				$103	29
					Dec.	2	By Bal. from old a/c	$ 10	65

[*Original in German*]

Paris,
11 Jan. 1870
6 Place St. Michel 6

DEAR MR. NALTNER!

My former wife has, against all expectations, sent a lawyer from [St.] Petersburg to Paris to file her suit against me. However, the local court did not accept the suit because I am an American citizen. Now it seems apparent that she will request copies of the proceedings of my divorce in Indianapolis through the International Bureau of Lawyers in New York or the Russian Ambassador in Washington. It is even possible that she will file suit to get the divorce annulled.

However this is not possible according to the laws of Indiana, because the divorce is . . . [illeg.] irrevocable.

Nevertheless, I kindly ask you to get the 3 Russian letters of my wife, with their translations, out of court and keep them for me.[45] In my opinion, the translations of 2 letters are not very accurate; in Russian, it always says that my wife will *never* follow me in *foreign countries* but there is nothing mentioned about America. . . .

[*Original in German*]   Paris,
                                                   21, January, 1870

DEAR MR. NALTNER!

Please see to it that as soon as you get notice directly from [St.] Petersburg or through the Russian Embassy in Washington or the International Lawyers Office in New York, please find out in the Marion Court of Common pleas in Indianapolis if a suit is filed against my divorce or if somebody is seeking information, and please make the necessary confirmation that I am a permanent citizen of Indianapolis and that I own a house at 473 [471] Illinois Street. If necessary you can prove, through my letters from New York that I live in New York during the cold winter months because I am afraid that my wife who was born in the hot south, could not take that terrible cold winter in Indianapolis, but that I intend to come back at the beginning of March. I also sent a letter to that effect to Hendricks, Hord & Hendricks, dated from New York, and send them the Warranty Deed of my provided house. Please see to it that these friends furnish in court as soon as possible my letter from New York and the Deed of my house and the personal proof that I am a permanent citizen of Indianapolis . . . .

[*Original in English*]   Athens in Greece,
                                                   23 March 1870

MESSRS. HENDRICKS, HORD & HENDRICKS INDIANAPOLIS

Dear Sirs!

I wrote to you in January last from New York that I hoped to return home to Indianapolis in a few weeks.

But unfortunately my wife fell so sick in the beginning of last month that, by the advice of the physician, I have been obliged to go with her to the celebrated sulphur-baths of this city.

She is fast getting better here but I now hardly hope to be back to Indianapolis before end of May next.

In my above letter I have sent you the registered deed of my house on Illinois street which I beg you to keep for me in your safe until I come

58   45 These letters are given below, pp. 65–68.

myself. Messrs. A. Seidensticker & Co. are receiving for me the monthly rent on that property.

Believe me to remain, Dear Sirs, yours faithfully,

HY. SCHLIEMANN

[*Original in English*]   Paris, 28 June 1870
                                                                    6 Place St. Michel

My dear Mr. Naltner!

I had very great pleasure in receiving the other day on my return from the Orient your esteemed lines of 18th May for I see that yourself and family are enjoying excellent wealth and that your business is steadily increasing. . . .

I rejoice to hear that Indianapolis is fast increasing in wealth and gigantic enterprises and I have not the slightest doubt that in consequence of its central position, its beautiful climate and the exuberant richness of the surrounding country, nay of nearly the whole state of Indiana, Indianapolis will become in the course of time one of the largest and most wealthy city of the Union.[46]

I would have come long since to Indianapolis with my good wife but unfortunately she has been dangerously ill for the last 3 months and has not even been able to accompany me to Paris, whither I was called by urgent business. I have been obliged to leave her with her parents at Athens and having finished my business here I return tomorrow night to the Orient in order to continue the excavations which I have very successfully begun in April last in ancient Troy. If my wife feels strong enough she will accompany me to those diggings but, alas, our journey to Indiana is out of the question until her health is most perfectly restored.

With sincere wishes for your and your dear family's prosperity I remain with hearty greetings for all

Yours very faithfully

H. SCHLIEMANN

[46] In his letter of May 18, Naltner had written: "Business in Indianapolis is flourishing, and a great many large Manufacturies are being built this summer. We enlarged the National Hotel and it is doing a good business in the hands of a new firm. The Wheeler and Wilson Sewing Machine Company have erected a new Manufactory here which will employ several hundred hands. There is a new Foundry being built which will take in four acres of Ground. Just north of the Post Office they have bought the whole block torn down the Houses thereon and are digging the celler for the new Hotel which will have eighteen Parlors and cost a quarter of a Million of dollars. All the dwelling Houses are occupied and there would be no trouble of renting more if they were only built up. There are now a great many business men from the east coming to Indianapolis and investing here. . . ." The new hotel referred to was the Denison, built at the southeast corner of Pennsylvania and Ohio streets, which was razed a few years ago. The Post Office was on the southeast corner of Pennsylvania and Market streets.

[Original in English]

TO CHARLES PARSONS, ST. LOUIS[47]

Athens in Greece
1 Feby. 1871

My dear Sir:

It is twenty months since I had not the pleasure of hearing from you, but I hope that you and your good Lady are enjoying good health.

I was in hopes you would come to Paris in the winter of 1869 to 1870, but no doubt your superior genius foresaw the present unlucky war and you quietly remained at St. Louis.

I remember with delight the happy hours I passed with you in 1869, when on my way to Italy, and later in Paris and nothing can give me greater pleasure than to hear of your and your good Lady's welfare.

I shall also be happy to hear that your sister in Law in Calcutta is doing well.

Ever since last spring I have been occupied with archeological researches in the Orient and particularly in the Plain of Troy, where I have discovered the Palace of Priamus and the Temple of Plinius Minerva. It is more than probable that I shall henceforward spend the most part of my time in excavations in Greece and Asia Minor and remain only three months yearly at Paris.

I wish therefore to have here a dwellinghouse and garden and have already bought here on the principal street a piece of ground of abt 2400 greek [?] . . . which I think corresponds to abt 2000 square yards, with an old building, which I intend to take down in order to rebuild it in the american style, for of all the elegant and comfortable houses I ever saw I must give the palm to those of the U.S. I should therefore feel immensely obliged to you if you would kindly send me at your earliest convenience the plan of a fine specimen of a St. Louis two story private dwelling house of abt 12 or better say 14 rooms, with water conduits and bathroom, such as I saw in that part of your town called St. Lucas I think. When at St. Louis three years since I have quite fallen in love with the american inner-shutters, which are used instead of curtains and which so convenient that I am sure they would be at once universally adopted in this country if I introduced them here. But since they are a thing unknown in this part of the world I should thank you to give me an exact drawing and measurement of them and to state of what wood they must be made. I suppose your windows have besides those outside shutters called in french—persiennes. Your plans will of course indicate how the roof is being made and how much it must project, further how the balconies are to be arranged? Marble being very cheap here I could make the colonnades of this material. Would it not be wiser to build the house immediately on the street

[47] See above, p. 51n.

—for then the garden becomes larger. Please inform me also how much such a house would cost at St. Louis?

For the trouble to make the plan please pay your architect one hundred francs, which I shall gratefully refund to you.

I intend leaving on the 4th inst for Paris in order to bring some order into what God may have saved of my houses and I therefore beg you will kindly send me your esteemed answer, with the plans and all particulars, care of my old friends Messrs. J. Henry Schroder & Co. of London.

I beg to thank you in anticipation most cordially for any trouble you may take in this matter and I assure you at the same time that it would give me immense pleasure to be able to serve you in return.

I remain with sincere regards My dear Sir yours very truly

HY SCHLIEMANN

My humble respects to Mrs. Parsons and Mrs. Mackay
[Charles] Parsons Esq. St. Louis

[Original in English]   Athens in Greece,
                                                              16 Sept. 1871

MESSRS. HENDRICKS, HORD & HENDRICKS INDIANAPOLIS
Dear Sir

It is two years since I left our good city of Indianapolis and in spite of my great desire to return there I have as yet been unable to do so, for I have entered into an agreement with the turkish government to excavate the Pergamus of Priamus on the site of Ancient Troy on the Hellespont and these excavations may still retain me in the Orient till next spring. But I intend returning then to Indianapolis in order to leave it no more.

In January 1870 I sent you for safe-keeping the title to my house on Illinois Street and I beg you will keep that document for me until my arrival with . . . [M.S. illeg.] Messrs. A. Seidensticker & Co., . . . [M.S. illeg.] hands on this property.

You remember that you obtained a divorce for me 30 June, 1869 and until now my first wife has not in the least molested me on that grounds. But now all at once she files here a complaint against me for bigamy. I have at once presented the copy of the judgment of divorce together with my other papers of citizenship. But my lawyer here in order to be able to refute at once all the charges against me desires to receive from you a document prepared and duly signed by your firm, in which you give explicit answers to the following questions: 1) "What were the form of methods prescribed by the laws, which were in force in Indiana in June 1869, to notification to a party residing in a foreign country that a complaint for divorce had been filed against him in any city of Indiana?
2) was a mere publication in the State Journal considered sufficient by the Law?
3) is a judgement given by default full powered by itself and can it not be   61

obtained even if it has . . . [illeg.] notified? Or does the law require that the judgement for divorce given by default must be notified to the other party.

4) in the latter case what are the proceedings to be prescribed to notify a similar judgement to a person residing in a foreign country and what rules delays which have appeared to raise opposition and to appeal against said judgement by default?"

You are very much requested to answer explicitly to these questions . . . them and to send on together with your consultation a copy of *the law which was in force at that time concerning divorce* and *also a copy of the articles of the Indiana civil rule concerning the proceedings in such divorce cases.* Of course I speak only of the laws existing in June 1869.

You told me at that time that by the law of Indiana Statutes, Article [XXVIII], Section [DLXXXVI] no complaint for a review of a judgement of divorce could ever be filed[48] and further that I had no necessity to notify the judgement to my divorced wife and I hope you can confirm that now.

I trust that you will not be delayed in your promise to write me the above document the more so since I only . . . [illeg.] to state the sacred truth. Please write me at the same time what your fee is for the document in question and the copies of . . . [illeg.] of the divorce law and I promise to send you that fee at once, in a bill on New York.

Please address your letters simply, M. Henry Schliemann, Athens, Greece.

I am with sincerity and truthfulness

H. SCHLIEMANN

[*Original in English*]

Athens in Greece,
3 Decb. 1871

MESSRS. HENDRICKS, HORD & HENDRICKS INDIANAPOLIS
Dear Sirs

In the excavation of Ancient Troy, with which I have been busy for 2 months, I had the pleasure to receive your esteemed favor of 12th Oct. and I would hasten to beg you will accept the expression of my warmest thanks for having so promptly attended to my request. At the same time I beg leave to enclose a bill on New York for $50. for the trouble I have given you.

But I am now happy to inform you that my first wife merely intended to threaten me with a law-suit and that she has 3 weeks ago obtained in the court of St. Petersburg her divorce in *full* form so that, even

[48] See above, p. 22.

by the laws of Russia, everything is now finished between her and me and no lawsuit can ever take place between us.

I remain very respectfully your obedt servt

H. SCHLIEMANN

[*Original in English*]
Athens 3 Decb. 1871

Ccy $50.

At Sight please pay against this my assignment to the order of Messrs. Hendricks, Hord & Hendricks the sum of Fifty Dollars Currency and debit me the same H. SCHLIEMANN

MESSRS. L. VON HOFFMANN & CO. NEW YORK

[*Original in English*]
private
Athens in Greece,
3 Dec. 1871

MESSRS. HENDRICKS, HORD & HENDRICKS INDIANAPOLIS
Dear Sir

My property in Indianapolis, of which you hold the title papers, is so small that it is not worth my while to keep it. . . .

I therefore beg you will kindly sell the property, either by public auction or by private contract, just as you think is best in my interest. It cost me $1100. and besides $27.50 brokerage. But I give you no limit and only beg you will take care of my interest as if it were your own.

The proceeds of the sale, after deducting your charges and Commission, pray remit for my account to Messrs. L. von Hoffmann & Co. of New York.

I beg leave to hand you enclosed full power for the sale and transfer. I know that the sale of property is not your business, but nevertheless I trust that you will not refuse to sell this . . . [illeg.] do it. If however for reasons unknown to me you cannot do it yourselves I beg you will kindly entrust the sale to a party in whose ability and integrity you have implicit confidence.[49]

I remain . . .

H. SCHLIEMANN

[49] For the sale of Schliemann's South Illinois Street property, see above, p. 21n.

[*Original in English*]

Troy in Asia Minor,
1 April 1873

MESSRS. HENDRICKS, HORD & HENDRICKS INDIANAPOLIS
Dear Sirs

By the present I beg you will kindly hold at the disposal of Messrs. L. von Hoffmann & Co., of New York the title deed and other papers you may hold of my house in Illinois street, and transfer to the person or persons they may indicate the full-power I sent you in the beginning of last year for the sale of the house. Any charges there may be said friends will pay you.

Since the 1st February I am here again with 150 labourers busily engaged in excavating the Pergamus of ancient Troy, and, I am happy to say, the result far exceeds my most sanguine hopes.

I am Dear Sir Yours very faithfully

H. SCHLIEMANN

LETTERS OF CATHERINE SCHLIEMANN TO HER HUSBAND
Presented to the Marion County Court of Common Pleas with the Petition for Divorce

[From copies in English translated from the originals in Russian][1]

18, March, 1868

MY DEAR HUSBAND:

I have delayed the answers to your various letters for I was required some time for reflection. You continually insist upon it & desire energetically I should follow you with our children to America and live there conjointly with you. You further ask my advice how to convey your ready cash and how I think of [illeg.] the purchase of real estate in the U. S. In answer to this I can merely repeat what I have told you a thousand times both verbally and by letter, viz. *that not only I energetically refuse to live with you in a foreign country wherever it may be, but that I also peremptorily refuse to leave Russia even for the shortest time.*

Regarding investments of money you are a better judge than I & you have made your whole fortune yourself and by the laws of Russia I have no share in your fortune except what you may bequeath to me in your last will. I rest therefore as you think safe and best.

Your devoted wife

C. SCHLIEMANN

18 April 1868

MY HUSBAND!

The tenor of your last letters is not very amiable, but since you do not use [illeg.] Russian language, I reply you and repeat to you again the reason which prompt me to act against your desire. Consider my situation and the cause of all our displeasure. *The sole* and only reason of all our disagreement is that you desire I should leave Russia and join you in

---

[1] Transcribed from photostatic copies of the English translations which are in the Schliemann papers. The transcriptions were made by Mrs. Eva Rice Goble and Miss Diana Goble.

America. But this I most decidedly decline and refuse to do and I assure you with a [illeg.] at oath, that for nothing in the world I shall ever leave Russia and that I would sooner die than live together with you in a foreign country. Thus my opposition to your desire is called by you caprice and fanaticism. I have always endeavored to fulfil your desires, whereas this time I cannot give way and most tenaciously insist upon my will, because here the education of our children is compromised in which uncertainty and inconstancy is inadmissible.

I remain your devoted wife

C. SCHLIEMANN

31 Decbr. 1868

MY HUSBAND:

Your last two letters I have left for a long time unanswered because their contents have struck and astonished me too much and for a long time I did not know what to answer. You continue to torment me with your request to emigrate with our children to the U.S. in order to live there together with you; you talk of this emigration as if it were easy to accomplish. You consider this emigration as a certainty, whilst in spite of all your endeavours, throughout two years and a half to persuade me you have not yet seen on my part the slightest sign of consent. I hope you remember that at our marriage no condition was made that I should ever leave St. Petersburg. Finally, what would become of our son Sergius? You wish he should be educated in America in order that he might later become administrator of your immeasurable property and I confess his fate would not be an object of envy! Do you then indeed not think that one can give the children in St. Petersburg as good an education as in America and particularly so if one has ample means? I feel much astonished at your apprehension that our son should learn dissipation in the Russian schools. I think if a man dissipates his fortune, the schools cannot be the cause of it. I do not know . . . [illeg.] if american schools . . . [illeg.] education for dissipation. If some from russia . . . [illeg.] how to preserve their . . . [illeg.] and if they give thoughts no less to dissipation and . . . [illeg.] the cause of it ought to be looked for . . . [illeg.] life.

But I have . . . [illeg.] not heard that there was more . . . [illeg.] in the U. S. than elsewhere in the world. Infinitely better is it that Sergius should finish his education in St. Petersburg. At the age of 13 one cannot send him from one country to the other without doing injury to his whole being; he would thus never get accustomed to any one country. Irrevocably he would lose the love for his mother country, your . . . [illeg.] idea holds too lightly. The schools are here as good as anywhere else. If some objects of instruction are but poorly presented, then we have the means to supply the deficiency by private lessons. After having finished the courses of instruction here in the gymnasium he can always pass over to the highest institutions of learning in America or in Germany —according to circumstances. Besides I see neither cause, nor reason, nor desire [?] why we should emigrate to the U. S. although you possess there a good deal of real estate, yet you are not obliged nor forced to reside there.

I therefore reiterate to you for the thousandth time that I oppose myself in the most decided way and in the most peremptory manner to live together with you in America or wherever it may be outside of Russia, and, in order that you may not torment me any more on this head I herewith swear a solemn oath that I shall never pass the Russian frontier.

Niederhiffer [?] has the consumption and his days are counted. I hardly think he can live until next summer but I have already got a place for his wife as governess with my brother.

This winter is remarkably cold and for some days even the quicksilver in the thermometer was frozen so that we could not see what the exact temperature was. Many people are frozen to death in the cars of the Moscow railway, because unfortunately they have not introduced yet on our railroads the American system of heating the cars. Now there is some appearance of a change in the weather.

I have for the . . . [illeg.]

Your devoted wife

C. SCHLIEMANN

ST. PETERSBURG,
16 Feby 1869

MY HUSBAND!

I have received your letters of 14th, 17th, 20th, 23d inst and resume their long contents in the following points:

1/ You demand that I should leave my mother country. 2/you demand that I should prevail upon my children to do the same and that I should deprive them of the great blessing to be educated in the orthodox religion. You endeavor to persuade me to do this, now with threats of the police, of poverty or of forfeiture of inheritance, now again by promises of luxury, of pleasures and of immense inheritance to my children. To all this I answer briefly.—I hope that the police will lend their assistance to me and not to you, because my desires and demands are just, honest, disinterested and lawful, whereas yours are perfectly in opposition to the laws and religion of my mother-country. Poverty and deprivation of inheritance are, I confess, very hard to me, but should such take place, then, I feel assured, to look down on them from the summit of your wealth will be still more painful to you and your remorse will be the best compensation for such acts of yours. You are aware that I have never sought for luxury, and you have neither accustomed me to it. I can do without it very well. I have neither sought for pleasure, being always contented with my family circle. Whether my children will be rich heirs or not, that only God knows. I pray to him for one thing only, that he may give me the strength and the possibility to educate and to form our children so that they do honour to your name. Fortune in this world is only in that case agreeable and useful when it is employed wisely and usefully and with real profit to one self and to others; but at all events it is only then agreeable when one has the free disposal of it and if one has not to submit for its sake to a limitation of ones personal liberty, in the shape [?] as you want to oblige our children not to submit . . .

DR. SCHLIEMANN'S WILL AND PROBATE RECORD, Marion County, Indiana.

Will Record FF page 190 Filed January 4, 1922

HENRY SCHLIEMANN   *Will*

No. 76086. A Translation from the French language
An Extract: ————

No. 61198—A Translation from the Greek language.

On the tenth of January, in the year One thousand eight hundred and eighty nine, I the undersigned, a citizen of the United States of America, Heinrich Schliemann, having my lawful residence in the City of Indianapolis, in the State of Indiana, United States of America, and living in Greece, in my house in Athens, having the enjoyment of all my faculties, I have made and written with my own hand my Will under the following paragraphs:

1: I constitute as my heirs my four children, to wit: Serge and Nadesche Schliemann which I got from a first wedlock and Andromaque and Agamemnon Schliemann which I got from my second wedlock.

2: I give to my son Serge Schliemann, born in September 1855, as his share in my inheritance, my house being the No. 7 in Aubirst street, Temple quarter, and my house bearing the No. 33 in Arcade street, Madeleine quarter, both of them in Paris, and furthermore a sum of Fifty thousand francs in cash and in gold.

3: To my daughter Nadesche Schliemann born in July 1861, I give as her share in my inheritance the house I am possessed of in Paris, bearing the No. 6 in the Calais street near Blanche Street and the estate I am possessed of and that bears the No. 161 in the Buchanan Street, Indianapolis,[1] furthermore a sum of Fifty thousand francs in cash and in gold—

The title deeds of the above-mentioned three buildings situate in

[1] In March, 1879, ten years after Dr. Schliemann's sojourn in Indianapolis, he acquired a house and lot in Indianapolis at what is now 829 (Old No. 161) East Buchanan Street. The price was $1,000, and the deed was acknowledged before Charles E. Coffin. The purpose of this purchase probably was to support Dr. Schliemann's American citizen-

Paris are deposited with the Notary Public Mr. Albert Laveine, of No. 13, Tartbuct Street, Paris, I add that such buildings are free of any debt. The title-deeds of the building in Indianapolis are in the same envelope as this my Will, this estate is likewise free of any mortgage.

4. Whereas these three houses in Paris are always well let and produce a fair income, I earnestly advise my son Serge and my daughter Nadesche to keep them up and leave the management of same to Polynice Beamain, of No. 25, Chaussee d'Antin Street, Paris who managed them ever since seventy-three years [1873?] to my entire satisfaction. Should my daughter Nadesche would be desirous to sell the Indianapolis estate, I recommend her to send a Power-of Attorney authenticated by the American Consul to my Bankers, Messrs. L. von Hoffmann & Co., New York City, who until the present time have managed same through their Indianapolis Agent.————

5: The address of my children Serge and Nadesche Schliemann is to be found at Messrs. L. E. Günzbourg's Bankers, of St. Peterborough———

6: I give as their share in my inheritance to my two other children Andromaque, born in May 1871 and Agamemnon, born in March 1878, all the residue of my personal and real estate which shall be found belonging to me at the time of my death, except, however, the house known under the name of "*Iliou Melathron*, Ilion Abode" and the piece of land which depends of same in University Street, Athens, whereas said house and garden as well as the furniture, library and antics which are therein with the exception of my antics trojan set, I gave them to my wife Sophia Schliemann, formerly Engastromenos by virtue of the gift-deed No. 31854 drawn up by the Notary Public Antoniades such document is to be found within the envelope containing the present Will. I give to my children Andromaque and Agamemnon the said share in my inheritance under the express condition they shall conscientiously deliver the particular legacies I make in my Will and that they faithfully shall pay to my children Serge and Nadesche the sums in cash I leave to the latter————

7: Catherine, born Lyschin, was my first wife; I was compelled to part from her in June 1869 in Indianapolis, Indiana, under the divorce

ship. The legal description of the property is 30 feet off the east side of lot number 179 in Dougherty's subdivision of outlot 99. The transaction is noted in Deed Record 121, page 471, dated March 7, 1879, and recorded the same day.

The affidavit of Edwin H. Forry appended to this will record, below, shows that Nadesche (Nadezhda) Schliemann, to whom the place was devised in her father's will, had become Nadesche Androussoff by marriage. She became a refugee during the First World War, and was finally located in Paris by the Indianapolis bank in 1921. Taxes on the house and lot became delinquent and the property finally was sold by Marion County in January, 1958.

There is no house on the lot now, but it is remembered by an elderly neighbor as

the place formerly owned by "that Russian who went away and never came back."

deed enclosed to which is attached my American citizen diploma. I leave to the said Catherine, born Lyschin a sum of One hundred thousand francs in cash and in gold. Her address is to be found at Messrs. Günzbourg's, Bankers, of St. Petersborough——

8: For the maintenance and education expenses of Andromaque and Agamemnon, I allow for each of them until they are of age, seven thousand francs in gold a year——

(Seal)

I have executed and written by my own hand this Will in Athens, on the tenth day of January, in the year One thousand eight hundred and eighty-nine——

(Signed) Henry Schliemann

Published and proved under a resolution of the Court of First Instance in Athens issued under No. 9435 of the current year——Athens, this eighteenth (18) day of December 1890 (ninety)——[Julian Calendar]

——By the President

——(Signed) Th. Pharangos

——Judge—

"I, the undersigned, a Sworn Translator to the Court of Appeal, Paris, France, do hereby certify the foregoing to be a true and faithful translation from its original in French language which exists on pages 1 to 5, and 17 of same, as initialled, the said original signed "Ne Vaneten" under No. 76086 at the date hereof.

Paris, August 8th, 1921
G. Collet.   (Seal)

VU AU GREFFE
G. Lozt.

Vu pour la legalisation de la
signature de M. Collet
Traducteur juré prés la Cour
d'Appel de Paris
apposée ci-demis
Paris, le 10 Août 1921.
Pour le Premier President,
L. L. Tuey.

Estate Docket 62 page 19747

THE PROBATE COURT OF MARION COUNTY
HENRY SCHLIEMANN   *Estate*

Jan. 4, 1922, Foreign will filed and ordered spread of record
Order Book 73 page 328.
(No further administration)

EDWIN H. FORRY   *Affidavit*

Affiant says that he was formerly Vice-President of The Central Trust Company, of Indianapolis, Marion County Indiana, and is now Vice-President of the Farmers Trust Company, of said City, County and State; that the former company, prior to its purchase by the latter company in 1913, had the rental of certain real estate known as 829[2] Buchanan Street, Indianapolis, Indiana; that the correct legal description of said property is:

Lot 179 in Dougherty's Subdivision of Out Lot 99 of the city of Indianapolis;

that the said real estate was owned by one Henry Schliemann at the time of his death; that by the terms of the will of said Henry Schliemann, a certified copy of which will is recorded in office of the Clerk of the Marion Probate Court, in Will Record FF, page 190, the property at 829 Buchanan Street, Indianapolis above described, was devised to Nadescha Schliemann, daughter of said testator; that for a number of years prior to 1915, said companies paid over the rental income from said property to one Nadescha Androussoff, who was then a resident of St. Petersburg, (Later Petrograd) Russia; that during the World War, no trace could be had of said Nadescha Androussoff but that in the year 1921, communication was again renewed, and upon proper verification by the Paris Branch of the Bankers Trust Company of New York City, a Russian Refugee by the name of Nadescha Androussoff was found to be the same person as Nadescha Schliemann, daughter of Henry Schliemann, and said Farmers Trust Company accordingly paid over to said Nadescha Androussoff the rental income from said real estate at 829 Buchanan Street; that this affiant has seen a certified certificate of the marriage of Nadescha Schliemann to one Nicholas Androussoff, and is satisfied that Nadescha Schliemann, daughter of Henry Schliemann, and devisee under his will to the property at 829 Buchanan Street Indianapolis, Indiana, is the same person as Nadescha Androussoff, whose present residence is 5-G Bd. Malesherbes, Paris, France, and that said affiant has communicated with said Nadescha Androussoff at said address on numerous occasions during the past year relative to said real estate.   EDWIN H. FORRY

[2]Old No. 161.

The State of Indiana   *Tax Deed*
(Seal)
By E. Allen Hunter,
Auditor Marion County,
Attest: C. S. Ober,
Treasurer Marion County to Marion County
    30 Ft. E. Side Lot 179 in Dougherty's Sub. OL 99.

    Returned delinquent in the name of Henry Schliemann for the non payment of taxes, costs and charges for 1955 and prior years and bid in by Marion County, Ind. on December 3rd. 1956 and Certificate No. 91385 issued therefor.

Archaeological Phase

It would have taken a bold and optimistic person to have foretold success for the marriage of this inexperienced seventeen-year-old Greek girl, Sophia Engastromenos, with a hard-driving, eccentric international merchant of almost three times her age. However, bound together by strong personal regard, love of Greece, her history, literature, and tradition, it may be truly said that they came very close to living happily ever after. Both being persons of spirit, an occasional spark would fly, but like those from a blacksmith's anvil they did not burn.

Sophia always stood loyally by her husband and in difficult situations would always say the appropriate soothing words at the proper time. She really dominated him without his knowing it. Her intuitive knowledge of human nature and her gracious manner dispelled the threatening clouds that would gather around Schliemann and those who stood between him and his unflagging faith in Homer. He, with many other scholars, has held Homer to be the moulder of the Greeks and since their influence on the rest of Europe down through the ages was so profound, was he not right in his superlative admiration for the blind poet?

On his part, Schliemann, as far as his nature would permit, loved her sincerely and served her with the best intentions he could muster. He always acknowledged his debt to her for invaluable help and co-operation and proudly enjoyed the appreciation of her by others.

They were married on September 24, 1869, and immediately set out for Paris via Naples, Pompeii, and Florence. Arriving in the French capital, they occupied a palatial apartment overlooking the stone-walled and wooded banks of the Seine and in view of the dark towers of Notre Dame. There they were saddened by the news of the death of Sophia's father and of Heinrich's older daughter Natalya and by the ill effects of the Parisian climate on Sophia's health. On the advice of her doctors they returned to Athens in April, 1870. Schliemann, himself, made a brief visit to several islands in the wine-dark waters of the Aegean Sea.

77

Being impatient to begin the work of revealing Troy to the world, and with no authority from anyone, he started a small army of men digging a large trench in the northwest edge of the dry, barren, windy hill of Hissarlik. The owners, two voluble and gesticulating Turks, immediately made trouble, but a small payment and the privilege of selling the excavated stone to near-by villagers, secured a truce until that trade languished. Then the work was stopped and Schliemann angrily and reluctantly returned to Athens.

He was destined to suffer most from two sets of circumstances during the archaeological phase of his life; difficulties with Turkish and Greek "Ministries of Red Tape and Sealing Wax" over authority to conduct excavations, and the prevailing lack of a recognized technique for adequately digging and recording his discoveries. He had to develop his own methods through a painful period of teething troubles. These procedures were constantly being improved during the years, for he was always willing to learn. The majority of savants who had done little themselves to improve the situation, continually belittled his "unscientific" work. It was years before he was able to reduce their opposition to pulp.

On August 12, 1871, the proper *firman* permitting further exploration at Troy was finally received from the Turkish government which, in the meantime, had purchased the land belonging to the two recalcitrant Turks. Isaac Wayne MacVeagh, American minister to Turkey, had been of assistance in obtaining the permit.

While he had been waiting for the *firman* his daughter Andromache had been born in Athens. The Franco-Prussian war was raging and Schliemann had also been in Paris to assure himself of the safety of his property during the siege by the Germans, passing through their lines with a forged passport. Early in the year, too, he had applied to Athens for the right to explore Mycenæ but was denied the privilege on the ground that there were dangerous banditti in the region.

The Schliemanns arrived in the Troad late in September, and in their work were subjected to the violent white light of the sun with its sizzling heat, to drenching rains, icy cold, eternal winds, and dust. They toiled all day unearthing walls, stone-age artifacts, black obsidian knives, and terra cotta objects, writing up their records at night. Bad weather forced their return to Athens in November.

In the following year, 1872, work at Troy began in March with 160 workmen outfitted with excellent tools and supplies furnished by Schliemann's old friend Schröder from his London branch. Huge walls and marble slabs were found but the *piece de resistance* was a large relief of Apollo as the sun god. This was smuggled out of the country and in later days it graced the verdant garden of the discoverers. Fever and storms drove them back to Athens just as some gold rings had been found. Upon returning later, they caught the watchmen selling the excavated stone!

Schliemann made an offer to the Greek government to excavate Mycenæ and Olympia at his own expense and to build a public museum, costing 200,000 francs, to house the material. It was to become the property of the nation upon his death. The offer was refused.

His *firman* to explore Hissarlik was canceled for a time but upon its renewal he began active work on the last of January, 1873, upon what was to be the most rewarding year at Troy.

He reported that 250,000 cubic meters of earth had been removed and soon an open space was uncovered which he at once mistakenly recognized as the famous Scæan gate of the *Iliad*. Not far from this, just below a part of a wall, the glimmer of gold was seen through a narrow slit. A holiday, "his birthday," was quickly announced to get rid of the workmen and guards and he and Sophia secretly and carefully removed the treasure. Its richness surpassed all belief; golden diadems—one composed of ninety chains of rings, twenty-four bright gold necklaces, gleaming goblets, countless earrings, and other objects to a total of eight thousand. There were silver talents and vases, together with curious pieces of copper, and several vessels and bases of helmet crests, of the same ruddy material. All this was gathered into Sophia's large red shawl, sent promptly to the home of a friendly neighbor, and smuggled out of Turkey in the next few days.

Giving his imagination complete control Schliemann called this rich find "the treasure of Priam" and the stratum in which it lay "Troy." As a matter of fact, it came from a much older layer than Homer's Troy, and in after years his good friend William Dörpfeld proved that Schliemann had never seen the real Troy. Where he dug the most romantic stratum had been removed for the construction of another town. The subsequent discoveries of the enthusiast at Mycenæ and Tiryns led to the recognition of Homer's city, after his death. It is presently identified as level VIIa, a decision strengthened by the work of the University of Cincinnati expedition headed by Professor Carl W. Blegen.[1]

The *firman* called for an equal division of objects found between Turkey and the archaeologist. Schliemann justified himself for taking it all by claiming that the Turks had broken so many terms of the agreement that it was no longer binding. He also claimed that the Ottoman share would simply have been melted up for its intrinsic value.

Such a find was sure to cause rumors and gossip and resulted in government officials going to the extreme of searching the Schliemann premises but, of course, they found nothing. The Turks sued—and much time in the following year was taken in fighting the case through the lower and upper courts. The Greek judge finally found in favor of Constantinople

[1] C. M. Bowra, "Homer's Age of Heroes," in *Horizon*, III, No. 3 (January, 1961), pp. 77, 84.

and fixed a fine of 50,000 francs which Schliemann regarded as a victory, for the treasure was worth several times that amount. He immediately sent a contribution of 250,000 francs to the museum in the Turkish capital.

During the trial, with the consent of Athens, he removed at his own expense an objectionable eighty-foot medieval tower from the Athenian acropolis.

These were difficult times for our friends for they had trouble, not only with the Turks but with the Greeks, and several cities, the police, and even their own lawyers.

Schliemann somehow found time to make some experimental trenches at Mycenæ, without the consent of the Greek authorities. For five days he dug unauthorized trenches within the acropolis instead of outside which the experts had always considered the more likely place. Again his interpretation of the descriptions of Pausanias was more correct than those of the smug professionals. Even though his work was stopped by the furious functionaries, he had discovered enough to encourage further effort. Within two months he had permission to continue operations.

The Schliemanns then took something of a respite from their labors and visited England where they won the friendship and moral support of Gladstone and then journeyed to Holland "to visit the Queene." From there, their travels took them to Copenhagen, Rostock, and Italy. Of course, musty museums and brilliant scientists were their chief interests.

The year 1876 brought to light the glittering treasures from the royal tombs of Mycenæ. This ancient city was second only to Troy in Greek literature and tradition, for it was the capital of the Atridae and the birthplace of Perseus. The tragic stories of Pelops, Agamemnon, Electra, Clytemnestra, and Ægisthus were centered within the dark walls. In the circular agora, not far from the famous Lion Gate, Schliemann and Sophia uncovered the famous five legendary royal tombs. Twelve chests they filled with bright golden booty, face masks, disks, girdles, plaques, goblets, diadems, and laurel leaves loaded with brilliant gems. There were eighty bronze swords, many with golden hilts, also lances and battle axes. Articles of radiant silver and translucent alabaster were also numerous.

Much of the delicate work of exhuming these precious and fragile articles fell to the lot of Sophia whose deft fingers preserved many of the pieces. Her charm and wiles were invaluable in dealing with the suspicious and officious inspectors.

Between exploration seasons the Schliemanns again visited Gladstone and foggy London where Sophia received an ovation after an address before the Royal Archaeological Society. In July, 1878, 190 house foundations were unearthed in the ancient capital of Odysseus and a sixth short

ILIOU MELATHRON,
The Schliemann Home in Athens

season at Hissarlik produced a relatively small cache of gold bars, spirals, rings, and heavy bracelets of electrum, along with a silver dagger. Schliemann was allowed to keep one third of these items according to the terms of the current *firman*.

By far the most important event of the time (1878) to Sophia and Heinrich was the birth of their son whom they christened with the royal name of Agamemnon.

The ensuing year was marked by the publication of the book *Ilios* and the strengthening of the priceless and sincere friendships of the pathologist Dr. Rudolf Virchow and the architect Dr. William Dörpfeld. Both of these men had been trained in science and were of immense help in improving and perfecting the technique of excavating, recording, and interpreting the finds.

The beginning of the 1880's saw the building and completion of the Schliemann mansion *Iliou Melathron* in Athens. It was indeed a palace. The internal arrangements, as might be expected, were most impressive and elegant and in perfect tune with the interests and eccentricities of the builders. It is said that on the walls of his study were views of New York and Indianapolis, two cities of which the builder had kindly memories. In his will, dated January 10, 1889, he recorded himself as a lawful resident of Indianapolis and a citizen of the United States. The palace was sold to the Greek government in 1926 to be used as the offices of the Supreme Court. The price was 27,000,000 drachmas.

Some excavations that were next made at Orchomenos did not reveal the gold treasure mentioned by Homer to be there. With Dörpfeld's aid an accurate map of the walls of Mycenæ was completed that season.

The choice of the final recipient of his prehistoric collection had worried Schliemann for some years. Would it be Greece, Italy, France, Germany, or England? At one time he had offered to sell the jewels of his treasures to Russia, but as his interest in various countries waxed and waned so did his favor swing from one land to another. Finally, as he and Virchow were discussing the subject, while seated high on the side of Mt. Ida overlooking the broad Troad, gazing at the hazy radiance enfolding the coastline with an opalescent sheen, his friend handed him a sprig of flowering buckthorn saying, "A nosegay from Ankershagen." These few words brought a rush of nostalgic memories to the aging archaeologist and he decided to present the collection to the German nation. Sophia would much rather have given it to Greece but finally acquiesced in its going to the Berlin Museum. The gift brought them both important honors but none so highly appreciated as honorary citizenship of the city of Berlin for Dr. Schliemann. Up until that time only Bismarck and Moltke had received such recognition.

The Trojan treasure remained in Berlin until the end of the Second **81**

World War when its hiding place was found by the Russians. No one has heard of it since.

One of the smaller excavations that Schliemann initiated was in the provocative mound at Marathon, said by Pausanias to contain the bones of many Athenians who died in that famous battle. No skeletal matter at all was revealed.

At Tiryns, the legendary birthplace of the mighty Hercules, the whole plan of an Homeric palace was laid bare. As mentioned previously, the disclosures made at Mycenæ and Tiryns afterwards were determining factors in the selection of the true Homeric Troy from among the other strata at Hissarlik.

Schliemann was to make two deluxe exploratory trips up the Nile before his death but the final phase of his life had begun and his divine fire was gradually being quenched. Several attempts to dig at Knossos in Crete were completely baffled by the chicanery of the landowner.

All during his life Schliemann had been a great believer in the efficacy of bathing in the salt water of the sea. It really amounted to a mania and eventually caused his death. During his last years he suffered from severe and very painful ear infections, doubtless caused by constant sea bathing. He finally went to Halle for an operation which was supposed to have been successful. Subsequent lack of instruction or care by the surgeons, or his refusing to take proper precautions, or a combination of reasons, caused his death. He collapsed on the streets of Naples on Christmas, 1890, while returning to his precious Sophia in their shining home in Athens. He died the next day.

On Sunday, January 4, he lay in state in the great hall of *Iliou Melathron* surrounded with fragrant and beautiful flowers and with a bust of Homer at the head of his casket. King George and Crown Prince Constantine of Greece came with wreaths to honor him and letters of sympathy poured in from all quarters of the world. None was more valued than that handwritten by the octogenarian Gladstone. Sophia set aside a generous sum to which was added 30,000 marks by the German chancellor for the continuation of his work.

In order to convince scientists of the validity of his claims for archaeological findings Schliemann had organized two international conferences at Troy, one in 1889 and the other the year after. At these gatherings, with the aid of Virchow and Dörpfeld, he convinced all but a very small school of small fish of the soundness of his conclusions. The opinion is now unanimous that he was the founder of modern archaeology.

Appendix

Appendix

LIST OF SCHLIEMANN LETTERS WRITTEN FROM INDIANAPOLIS

Pages in 1869 Copy Press Letter Book	Date in 1869	To Whom Addressed	Language in Which Written
1–2	April 7	Adolph Schliemann, Schwerin	German
3	April 7	Giesecke & Devrient, Leipzig	German
4–5	April 11	Giesecke & Devrient, Leipzig	German
6	April 11	M. Lenz, Paris	German
7	April 11	C. Reinwald, Paris	German
8–9	April 11	*Adolph Schliemann	German
10–11	April 11	*To Father *et al.* in Lyck	German
12–14	April 13	*Archbishop Theokletos Vimbos, Athens	Greek
15–18	April 14	*E. Egger, Paris	Greek
19–23	April 14	*Ernest Renan, Paris	French
24	April 14	*Frank Calvert, Dardenelles	English
25–26	April 14	*E. W. Schliemann, Bordeaux	English
27	April 14	W. Kuhse, Lyck	German
28	April 15	L. von Hoffmann, New York	English
29	April 15	Giesecke & Devrient, Leipzig	German
30	April 20	L. von Hoffmann, New York	English
35	April 20	P. Beaurain, Paris	French
37	April 20	M. Concierge, 6 Place St. Michel, Paris	French

*Indicates letters that have been included herein in whole or in part.

Pages in 1869 Copy Press Letter Book	Date in 1869	To Whom Addressed	Language in Which Written
38–39	April 20	H. Burger, Boitzenburg	German
40	April 22	E. W. Schliemann, Bordeaux	French
41	April 11–22	J. E. Günzburg	French
42–43	April 23	General Beauregard, New Orleans	English
43–44	April 23	W. Kuhse, Lyck	German
45–46	April 26	*Archbishop Theokletos Vimbos, Athens	Greek
47	April 26	*Archbishop Theokletos Vimbos, Athens	Greek
48–49	April 26	Col. John S. Preston, Lexington, Virginia	English
49–50	April 27	Charles Parsons, St. Louis	English
51	April 27	E. W. Schliemann, Bordeaux	English
51	April 27	W. Kuhse, Lyck	German
52	April 27	*Archbishop Theokletos Vimbos, Athens	Greek
53–54	May 1	*Adolph Schliemann, Schwerin	German
55	May 1	Joh. Diestel, Mecklenburg	German
56	May 1	Bachman, Rostock	German
57–58	May 6	Charles Parsons, St. Louis	English
59	May 8	A. P. Stewart, Lebanon, Tenn.	English
60	May 8	John D. Stewart, Memphis	English
61–62	May 10	Charles Parsons, St. Louis	English
63–64	May 10	Charles Parsons, St. Louis	English
64	May 10	C. Reinwald, Paris	French
65	May 10	C. Andrew, Neu Strelitz	German
66–67	May 13	L. H. Stewart, Memphis	English
68–71	May 13	Charles Rhodes, Oswego, N. Y.	English
72–74	May 15	*Isidoros Skilissis, Paris	Greek
75	May 15	L. von Hoffmann, New York	English
76–77	May 15	*J. H. Schröder, London	English

*Indicates letters that have been included herein in whole or in part.

Pages in 1869 Copy Press Letter Book	Date in 1869	To Whom Addressed	Language in Which Written
78–80	May 16	Charles Parsons, St. Louis	English
81–82	May 18	W. Kuhse, Lyck	German
83–84	May 18	*To Father, Schwerin	German
84	May 19	A. Schliemann, Schwerin	German
85	May 19	E. W. Schliemann, Bordeaux	English
86–87	May 20	Charles Rhodes, Oswego, N. Y.	English
88	May 20	*A. Seidensticker & Co., Indianapolis	English
90	May 20	Charles Parsons, St. Louis	English
91–93	May 20	*Abram W. Hendricks, Indianapolis	English
94–100	May 23	*Th. Thibaut-Brignolles, St. Petersburg	French
101	May 23	Sergius Schliemann, St. Petersburg	French
102	May 24	M. Lenz, Paris	German
102	May 24	J. E. Günzburg, St. Petersburg	German
103	May 26	P. Beaurain, Paris	French
104	May 27	Charles Parsons, St. Louis	English
105–10	May 29	*Dr. H. Drisler, New York	English
111–12	May 30	Dr. H. Drisler, New York	English
112–13	May 13	Charles Parsons, St. Louis	English
114–15	June 1	Th. Thibaut-Brignolles, St. Petersburg	French
116	May 31	Charles Rhodes, Oswego, N. Y.	English
117	June 1	L. von Hoffmann, New York	English
117	June 1	H. Petrowsky, Roebel, in Mecklenburg	German
118	June 8	E. W. Schliemann, Bordeaux	French
118–19	June 5	*L. von Hoffmann, New York	English
119	June 6	*E. W. Schliemann, Bordeaux	English
120	June 7	Adolph Schliemann, Schwerin	German

*Indicates letters that have been included herein in whole or in part.

Pages in 1869 Copy Press Letter Book	Date in 1869	To Whom Addressed	Languages in Which Written
121	June 7	Th. Thibaut-Brignolles, St. Petersburg	French
122–28	June 8	*E. Egger, Paris	Greek
129	June 10	P. Beaurain, Paris	French
130	June 12	Charles Parsons, St. Louis	English
131	June 18	E. Erlanger, Paris	French
132	June 18	Charles Parsons, St. Louis	English
133–34	June 20	*E. Egger, Paris	Greek
134–35	June 21	E. W. Schliemann, Bordeaux	English
135	June 22	P. Beaurain, Paris	French
136	June 24	L. von Hoffmann, New York	English
136	June 29	L. von Hoffmann, New York	English
137	July 1	*E. Egger, Paris	Greek
137	July 1	*Archbishop Theokletos Vimbos, Athens	Greek
137	July 1	E. W. Schliemann, Bordeaux	French
138	July 1	P. Beaurain, Paris	French
139–41	July 1	Catherine Schliemann, St. Petersburg	English
142–43	July 1	Sergius Schliemann, St. Petersburg,	French
143–45	July 4	Ed. Wirths, Bonn	English
145–47	July 4	Catherine Schliemann, St. Petersburg	Russian
147–49	July 4	Th. Thibaut-Brignolles St. Petersburg	French
149	July 5	Sergius Schliemann, St. Petersburg	French
150–52	June 30	*Antonios Amiras, St. Petersburg	Greek
152	July 11	*A. Seidensticker & Co., Indianapolis	English
153–154	July 11	*E. Egger, Paris	Greek
155	July 13	E. W. Schliemann, Bordeaux	English
155–56	July 16	*Charles Parsons, St. Louis	English

*Indicates letters that have been included herein in whole or in part.

SOURCES ON DR. SCHLIEMANN'S LIFE AND WORK

"Dr. Schliemann: His Life and Work," in *Harper's Magazine*, LXVIII (1884), 898–904.

Gardner, Percy, "Henry Schliemann," in *Macmillan's Magazine*, April, 1891.

Hardy, Edmund, *Schliemann und Seine Entdeckungen auf der Baustelle des Alten Troja* (A. Foesser, Frankfurt, 1882).

Ludwig, Emil, *Schliemann, The Story of a Gold-Seeker*, translated from the German by D. F. Tait (Little, Brown & Co., Boston, 1931).

Mylonas, George E., *Ancient Mycenae: the Capital City of Agamemnon* (London, Routledge & Kegan Paul, 1957).

Payne, Robert, *The Gold of Troy. The Story of Heinrich Schliemann and the Buried Cities of Ancient Greece* (Funk & Wagnalls Company, New York, 1959).

Schliemann, Heinrich, *Briefwechsel, aus dem nachlass in auswahl herausgegeben von Ernst Meyer. I. Band von 1842 bis 1875* (Verlag Gebr. Mann, Berlin, 1953).

————, *Abenteuer meines Lebens . . . Selbstzeugnisse*, Hrsg. und erläutert von Heinrich Alexander Stoll (F. A. Brockhaus, Leipzig, 1958).

————, *Ilios, The City and Country of the Trojans . . .* (New York, Harper & Brothers, 1881).

————, *Mycenae, a Narrative of Researches and Discoveries at Mycenae and Tiryns . . .* (New York, Scribner, Armstrong & Co., 1878).

————, *Troja, Results of the Latest Researches and Discoveries on the Site of Homer's Troy . . .* (New York, Harper & Bros., 1884).

————, *Troy and Its Remains . . .*, translated into English by L. Dora Schmitz and edited by Philip Smith (John Murray, London, 1875).

Schmidt, H., *H. Schliemann's Sammlung Trojanischer Altertümer* (1903).

Schuchhardt, C., *Schliemann's Excavations . . .* translated from the German by Eugénie Sellers (Macmillan and Co., London and New York, 1891).

Scott, John A., "Schliemann and Indianapolis," in *The Classical Journal*, XVII (1921–22), 404–6.

Weber, Shirley H. (ed.), *Schliemann's First Visit to America 1850–1851* (Harvard University Press, Cambridge, Mass., 1942).

ELBERT HUBBARD REFUTED

In the August, 1902, issue of *The Philistine,* Elbert Hubbard published as one of his "Little Journeys to the Homes of Famous People," a journey to the home of Pericles. As an introduction to this he devoted a few pages to Dr. Schliemann. The most charitable thing that can be said of that bit of writing is that his usual comment and satire ran away with him entirely, and we hope that his tongue was pushing hard at his cheek at the time.

For example, Hubbard wrote that in Indianapolis Heinrich Schliemann was a wholesale grocer, and also ran a "feed-barn, a hay-scales, a sommer-garten, and a lunch-counter"! The territory of his operations extended out from Indianapolis to Peoria, Illinois, and Xenia, Ohio. He also, says Hubbard, opened a real estate addition to the Hoosier capital. Hubbard then suggested what a wonderful thing it would have been if Dr. Schliemann had given his "Trojan" treasures to Indianapolis instead of "the city of Berlin," since he made most of his money in the former city.

How many misstatements can be crowded into three pages?

Elbert Hubbard (1856–1915) was born in Bloomington, Illinois. He founded The Roycroft Press in East Aurora, New York, based on the communal Kelmscott Press of William Morris in England. In 1894 he began the publication in monthly booklets of his "Little Journeys," being short biographies accompanied by "comment and satire." Then *The Philistine* appeared, an avant-garde magazine, followed by *The Fra,* another periodical, in 1908. In 1899 he wrote *A Message to Garcia,* his most famous piece of writing. He went down on the "Lusitania" on May 7, 1915. The "Pericles" journey may also be found in *Little Journeys to the Homes of the Great* (Memorial Edition. The Roycrofters, East Aurora, New York, 1928), pp. 11 ff.

John A. Scott refuted the Hubbard story in a brief article in *The Classical Journal* (XVII, 1921–22, pp. 404–6), entitled "Schliemann and Indianapolis."

THE HENRY D. PIERCE CONNECTION

Mrs. Frederic Krull, daughter of Henry D. Pierce and well versed in local history, is our authority for the information that her father, just starting on his career as a young lawyer, often rode horseback with Dr. Schliemann and did some of the detail work in his divorce proceedings.

That Dr. Schliemann did ride horseback is verified under two dates in his diary. On April 20, he wrote that he had given up riding for two hours in the morning as he had been doing for the last ten days, and on June 1, recorded that he was again riding every morning. (See above, p. 16.)

On searching for evidence to confirm Mr. Pierce's legal activity in connection with the divorce, we were given a momentary thrill by the entry in Dr. Schliemann's diary on May 17, that "Representative Pierce requested to lay them [the bills concerning divorce] on the table till the following morning," but, of course, this Representative Pierce proved to be Gilbert A. Pierce of Porter County. (See above, p. 18.)

Henry D. Pierce studied law in the office of his uncle, Thomas A. Hendricks, in 1861, according to John H. B. Nowland (*Sketches of Prominent Citizens*, Indianapolis, 1876, p. 383). In the Indianapolis *Directory* for 1869 the office of Henry D. Pierce was listed at 24½ East Washington Street, the same address given in that publication for the offices of the law firm of Hendricks, Hord and Hendricks, attorneys for Schliemann, and also for the other following lawyers: Reginald H. Hall, Frederick Rand, John W. Ray, Eli F. Ritter, William Irvin, Byron K. Elliott, and Charles L. Holstein.

Presently, evidence is lacking to prove that Henry D. Pierce knew Dr. Schliemann or was concerned with his divorce. It is to be hoped that proof of this interesting connection will be forthcoming.

Index

93

Mycenæ, 80; marriage to Catherine Lishin, 5-6; second and third visits to America, 7; books by, mentioned, 5, 7, 8, 37, 81; receives degree from University of Rostock, 8, 31; granted divorce, 8, 15, 21, 22-23n, 25, 48, 49, 50, 70-71; American citizenship, 8, 12, 25, 53, 69; diary, 11-23; in New York, 11-13, 23; on American enterprise, 4, 13, 18, 19, 21, 23, 27-28, 47; in Indianapolis, 13 ff.; rents house, 14, 27, 49, 54; hires legal counsel for divorce, 14-15, 25, 29, 34-35; rides horseback, 16, 20, 90; on immigrant population, 18, 21, 50; works against amendments to Indiana divorce law, 17, 18-19, 35-36; in Fort Wayne, 20-21; buys house on South Illinois Street, 21, 49, 58, 61; sale of, 21n, 63, 64; buys interest in starch factory, 21-22, 49-50; letters, 24-64; considers marrying Sophia Engastromenos, 31-32, 33-34, 37; payment for divorce to A. Seidensticker & Co., 37; on The Arabian Nights, 38-40; on method of study and teaching of foreign languages, 41-45, 47; regards Indianapolis as permanent residence, 50, 54, 58, 59, 61, 69; on explorations of North Pole, 51-52; marriage to Sophia Engastromenos, 54, 77; auction of household articles, 55; account with Seidensticker & Co., 57; action against divorce threatened, 57, 58, 61-62; divorce confirmed, 62-63; seeks information on house construction, 60; letters from wife Catherine, presented with petition for divorce, 65-68; will and probate record, 69-73; house on Buchanan Street, Indianapolis, 69-70n, 72, 73; in London, 80-81; builds *Iliou Melathron* 81; gives archaeological collection to Germany, 81; made honorary citizen of Berlin, 81; death, 82; founder of modern archaeology, 82.

Schliemann, Ludwig (Louis), brother of Heinrich, 5.

Schliemann, Nadezhda (Nadesche), daughter of Heinrich, 6; bequeathed Indianapolis property, 69, 70, 72.

Schliemann, Natalya, daughter of Heinrich, 6; death, 77.

Schliemann, Sergius (Serge), son of Heinrich, 6, 66; bequest to, 69, 70.

Schliemann, Sophia (Engastromenos), wife of Heinrich, 4, 21n, 31, 37, 47, 82; considered as possible wife by Heinrich, 31-32, 33-34, 37; marriage, 54, 77; illness, 60, 61, 77; aids in archaeological work, 78, 79, 80; visits London, 80-81; bequest to, 70.

Schmidt, Lorenz, 54.

Schröder, B. H., and Company, 5.

Schröder, J. H., letter to, 36-37.

Schröder, J. Henry, & Co., 59.

Seidensticker, A., & Co., 37; letter to, 49; Schliemann's account with, 57.

Seidensticker, Adolph, 14-15n.

Servants, domestic, employed by Schliemann, 14, 15-16, 18, 20, 24, 27, 36.

Skilissis, Isidoros, letter to, 34-36.

Starch factory, Schliemann buys interest in, 21-22, 49-50; opened by Naltner and Mueller, 55.

Suicides, in America, 50.

Tellkampf, Th., 12.

Thibaut-Brignolles, Edward, 40n-41n.

Thibaut-Brignolles, Th., letter to, 40-41.

"The Thousand and One Nights," 38-40.

Tiryns, 7, 79, 82.

Troy, excavations at, 3, 7-8, 59, 61, 62, 64, 78, 79-80; "treasure" from, given to Berlin Museum, 81-82.

Turkey, opposition of government to Schliemann's excavations at Troy, 78, 79-80.

Union Starch Factory, 22, 55n.

University of Rostock, 8, 31.

Vimbos, Theokletus, 6, 7; letters to, 25, 30-32, 32-33, 33-34, 48-49.

Virchow, Rudolf, 81, 82.

Will and probate record, of Schliemann, 69-73.

Wisconsin, 30.

Wishmeyer, Charles F., 22n.